blue skies green fields

blue skies green fields

A CELEBRATION OF 50 MAJOR LEAGUE BASEBALL STADIUMS

IRA ROSEN

GRAMERCY BOOKS
NEW YORK

For Judy, who hung in with . . .

Author's Note: Several old stadiums, including Griffith Stadium and League Park, are not included in this book simply because I could not find suitable images of them.

This 2006 edition is published by Gramercy Books, an imprint of Random House Value Publishing, by arrangement with Clarkson Potter/Publishers, a member of the Crown Publishing Group, both divisions of Random House, Inc.

Gramercy is a registered trademark and the colophon is a trademark of Random House, Inc.

Random House
New York • Toronto • London • Sydney • Auckland
www.randomhouse.com

Printed and bound in China

Interior design by Maggie Hinders

Library of Congress Cataloging-in-Publication Data

Rosen, Ira (Ira D.)
  Blue skies, green fields : a celebration of 50 major league baseball stadiums / Ira Rosen.
    p. cm.
  Originally published: New York : Clarkson Potter, 2001.
  ISBN 0-517-22715-0
  1. Baseball fields—United States. 2. Baseball fields—United States—Pictorial works. I. Title.
  GV879.5.R67 2006
  796.357'06'873—dc22

                                                        2005045963

10 9 8 7 6 5 4 3 2 1

Acknowledgments

This book would not have happened without the creative, editorial, and emotional support of my wife, Judy. Thank you. I love you, too.

Special thanks to my agent, Jo Fagan, who believed in my vision; and to my editor, Chris Pavone, who made it happen.

Thanks also to:

Lori Ames, public relations maven, for the inspiration.

Maggie Hinders for the excellent design, Marysarah Quinn for the art direction, and everyone else at Crown Publishers, especially John Groton, Katie Workman, Andrew Stanley, Andrea Rosen, Jill Flaxman, Liana Faughnan, and Derek McNally.

Ralph Muscarella for sharing his postcards.

Arline Beneway-Lugert, the world's most understanding mother-in-law.

Mom and Howard for believing in me.

John Beneway for the tech support and advice.

Larry Beneway for the hospitality and pep talk (am I tough enough?).

Billy Sample, an even better person than he was a ballplayer. Although he did hit .272 lifetime.

All of the nice folks in the art and framing industry who supported my work, especially Bruce Teleky and George Leeson (how 'bout them Giants?).

All of the accommodating public relations people with the teams: Rick Cerrone, Yankees; Jay Horwitz, Mets; Jim Schultz and Glen Serra, Braves; Bob Rose, Giants; Glenn Geffner, Padres; Grace Morino, Dodgers; Brian Bartow and Melody Yount, Cardinals; Rick Vaughn, Devil Rays; Debbie Kenney, Athletics; Tim Mead and Larry Babcock, Angels; Bob Crawford, Diamondbacks; Tyler Barnes and Hunter Logan, Tigers; Desta Kimmel, Astros; Tim Hevly, Mariners.

Maarten Cote and Kim Generals at Kodak, Fair Lawn, New Jersey.

John Castronovo and Peter Ciresa at TPI, Fairfield, New Jersey.

Everyone who shared ballpark memories with me.

To all those who aspire, the best advice I've gotten is from my high school baseball coach, Anthony Lagos, who, a long time ago, told me to "keep working at it."

Contents

Introduction

THE LOVE FOR THE GAME of baseball has been passed down through generations. Despite occasional problems, there are reasons why millions of fans still return to the ballpark. It's the way the game unfolds—leisurely, measured by innings, not by a time clock. It's watching the batter trying to accomplish what is said to be the single most difficult challenge in sports—to hit a baseball. It's being part of the crowd, coming together in a common cause—cheering for the home team. And it's recapturing the wonderful memory of seeing a Major League Baseball stadium for the first time—emerging from the ramp into the brilliant sunshine, the vast expanse of green grass lined so carefully with white chalk; seeing the thousands of people, the scoreboard, the dugouts, the players. These are indelible images. And this book is about recapturing those images.

Funny thing about stadiums—you're out in the fresh air, but you're really inside a building. You enter the park via a gate, walk through a tunnel, go up a ramp until you reach the top—and then you're outside again. Heady stuff. Someone once told me about his first game: He was nine years old and had watched baseball only on a black-and-white television, so he was shocked to see that the grass at Yankee Stadium was green.

Once inside the ballpark, you root for your favorite team, the essence of being a baseball fan. When I was growing up in the sixties, a team would be handed down to you, sort of like a birthright: Your father rooted for the Yankees, so you rooted for the Yankees. Everyone in the neighborhood pulled for the Yanks, and you pulled for the Yanks. In cities with more than one team, fan allegiance has always been complicated: In Chicago, for example, you can cheer for either the Cubs or the White Sox, but hardly anyone roots for both.

ix

Of course, following a baseball team is not always easy, especially if winning is your priority. The Boston Red Sox spanned four generations without winning a championship until their amazing game in 2004. The Cleveland Indians posted only six winning seasons in the thirty-two-years stretch beginning in 1961. But regardless of which team you follow or why, once you choose, it's in your blood; true fans always stick with their team.

Team allegiance aside, many fans have undertaken a quest to visit every Major League Baseball stadium. Some try to see their favorite team while traveling to the parks; others simply want to say they've done it, accomplished this quest not only to visit each ballpark but to recapture that magical first time again and again. To climb that ramp, glimpse the sliver of bright blue sky and emerald green grass, to emerge at the top, awestruck at the beauty and scope.

blue skies green fields

Arlington
Stadium

NOW DEMOLISHED, Arlington Stadium was built in 1964, with a seating capacity of about 10,000, to house the minor-league Dallas–Fort Worth Spurs. It was known as Turnpike Stadium during its minor-league days, until 1971, when the American League's Washington Senators, renamed the Texas Rangers, moved here for the 1972 season. They added a couple of decks plus a press box above home plate, increasing capacity to slightly over 35,000. But a minor-league ballpark it remained (despite further renovation in 1992 that increased capacity to 43,000): Seating was about as close to the action as at a minor-league game, with the exception of the top deck behind home plate. The food and parking were adequate—all in all, a cozy, even intimate, setting for a major-league game.

Arlington Stadium did not have the structural capacity to add luxury suites or other amenities, and toward the end, it seemed rather run-down. But until it was replaced in 1993 by Ballpark in Arlington, built a couple of blocks away, this funky, former minor-league ballpark was about as close as you could get to the action at any ballpark west of Wrigley Field.

I never saw any big-league park in person.

Waited till I made it, waited till I earned it,

so I could see it. Mine was Texas.

—KENNY ROGERS

- ◆ *Former home of the Texas Rangers*
- ◆ *Arlington, Texas: Collins Street, Copeland Road, Randol Mill Road, and Stadium Drive East*
- ◆ *Built 1964*
- ◆ *Opening Day, Minor League: April 23, 1965*
- ◆ *Opening Day, Major League: April 21, 1972*
- ◆ *Final Game: October 3, 1993*
- ◆ *Cost: $1.9 Million*
- ◆ *Total Renovation Cost: $19 Million*
- ◆ *Seating Capacity: 10,500 (1965); 35,185 (1972)*
- ◆ *Largest Crowd: 43,705 (July 23, 1983)*
- ◆ *Former Name: Turnpike Stadium, 1965–1971*
- ◆ *Replaced by Ballpark in Arlington, 1994*
- ◆ *Demolished 1994*

DIMENSIONS	LF	LCF	CF	RCF	RF
1993	330	380	400	380	330

WILLIE BLAIR "The first game, I was relieving at the time, so I didn't play in the first game I was on the roster. But what I remember about that game was, Nolan Ryan was pitching, and he was always my favorite player. He had a no-hitter through five innings, but they took him out 'cause it was kind of cold and it was the first game of the season."

MIKE CUBBAGE "[Arlington] was where I broke in. Billy Martin was my first manager, with the Texas Rangers in 1974. It was an old minor-league ballpark. It was a tough park on left-handed hitters 'cause the wind blew in from right field. Mike Epstein came down from the Senators and really hated the ballpark 'cause he used to hit a lot of high fly balls to right field, and the wind would knock 'em down. Jeff Burroughs, same way. He had power the other way, he'd hit balls to right center field that the wind would bring back into the ballpark."

Astrodome

THE ASTROS, Houston's 1962 National League expansion team, played their first three seasons as the Colt .45's in a minor-league park named for the team. But in 1965, the first of the domed ballparks, the Harris County Domed Stadium, was built and billed as the Eighth Wonder of the World. Originally, it featured clear glass roof panels and real grass, which was a remarkable endeavor. Unfortunately, the players couldn't see fly balls against the roof because of the sun glare, and the groundskeepers couldn't keep the grass alive. So the roof was made opaque by painting it white, and someone invented AstroTurf just in time for the team to continue playing there. Unfortunately, this innovation also gave birth to the ground-ball triple and the rug-burn diving catch, among other negatives. In 2000, the Astros moved to Enron Field, another in the current style of baseball-only, retro-looking downtown stadiums.

As far as stadiums built in the sixties go, the Astrodome held up well. It didn't have a retractable roof like those built subsequently in Toronto, Phoenix, or Seattle, but architecturally it was more interesting than most of the other fixed-dome facilities. And the upper-deck outfield seats were not usually filled, so their bright yellow-and-orange color added a bit of spark.

With the move of the NFL's Houston Oilers franchise to Tennessee, the Astrodome will join the ranks of demolished stadiums. Seems hard to believe that a stadium so radical in 1965 could be totally obsolete thirty-five years later.

LARRY DIERKER "The Colt .45's broke spring training in 1965 and came home to host the Yankees in an exhibition series to christen the Astrodome. We arrived at night, and the Dome was lit up—otherworldly. When I walked through the tunnel and looked across the expanse of the field and up at the roof, it was really breathtaking. I felt like I had walked into the next century—from pistols to spaceships, and from high school to the big leagues, in just one year. I was eighteen years old."

DON BAYLOR "Well, I grew up in Texas, so the first major-league stadium [I saw] was the Astrodome. The first year it opened, I went down, observed Johnny Callison standing kind of sideways, playing right field. You know, I had never seen anybody stand sideways. Everybody else kind of looks head-on. Then I kind of sauntered over to left field, and there was a big guy, about six foot seven, named Walt Bond, playing left field there—saw the size of his feet and I said, 'Well, I don't know if I'm going to be that big.' Always wanted to play at that level, so it was quite an experience for a young kid growing up as a football guy, wanting to be a baseball guy. So it made a big impression on me, just the Astrodome itself, all the things, how they tried to attract fans coming to the ballpark—they had the ushers and Astro-looking Astronauts. Colt .45's shooting off the scoreboard and those kinds of things."

ANDY PETTITTE "First one I ever saw was the Astrodome. I guess you get a little chill, thinking about maybe playing there one day."

DOUG DRABEK "The Dome was my first time, and I think walking into it, how big it seemed. The sound that the Dome made—you might not get that at an outdoor stadium."

I always dreamed one day of playing in the Astrodome. And that dream came true.

— RON GANT

- *Former home of the Houston Astros*
- *Houston, Texas: Route 610 and Kirby Street*
- *Built 1965*
- *Opening Day: April 12, 1965*
- *Final Game: October 3, 1999*
- *Cost: $35 Million*
- *Seating Capacity: 46,217 (1965); 54,816 (1990); 54,379 (1998)*
- *Largest Crowd: 53,688 (October 3, 1997)*
- *Formal Name: Harris County Domed Stadium*
- *Former home of NFL's Houston Oilers*
- *Baseball's first domed stadium, replaced by Enron Field, 2000*

DIMENSIONS	LF	LCF	CF	RCF	RF
(1965)	340	375	406	375	340
(1990)	330	380	400	380	330
(1993)	325	375	400	375	330

TODD KALAS (BROADCASTER) "First time I was ever in a major-league park was actually the Houston Astrodome, when my dad worked for the Astros. We moved from Houston when I was five or six years old, but I do remember the exploding scoreboard and all the excitement that went along with that. Everything was so bright and new, it was just such a huge facility. As a youngster, everything seems huge, but that was truly amazing, and my few recollections of that place were just of the immense size."

CHUCK KNOBLAUCH "I grew up in Houston, so I remember going to the Astrodome as a kid. . . . I remember the old scoreboard. I mean, now it's old, but then it was the scoreboard that they had with the bulls and the cowboys and the shooting off their guns and stuff like that. And I always had a good time. You'd always hope for a home run 'cause that's when they would light it up. . . . I was disappointed when they changed it."

MIKE SOWELL (AUTHOR) "As a teenager living in Houston, my friend and I periodically sneaked in to the Astrodome while it was under construction, giving us a true sneak preview of baseball's first futuristic ballpark. When the Dome was completed, I was on hand for the first game played indoors, a spring exhibition game on April 9, 1965, highlighted by Mickey Mantle hitting the first home run in the stadium. I returned for the first official indoor game on April 12, 1965, and watched the Phillies beat the Astros 2–0 behind the pitching of Chris Short . . . but the action on the field was overshadowed by the Astrodome itself. I particularly remember the players in batting practice hitting fungoes straight up in an effort to hit the roof (no one did at that time) and the spectacle of the exploding scoreboard with its six-shooters firing and the bulls stampeding. And who could forget the sight of the groundskeepers dressed in space suits as they raced out to drag the infield? . . . There was an atmosphere of excitement that seemed to feed on itself in what then was a spectacular structure, one worthy of its title as the Eighth Wonder of the World."

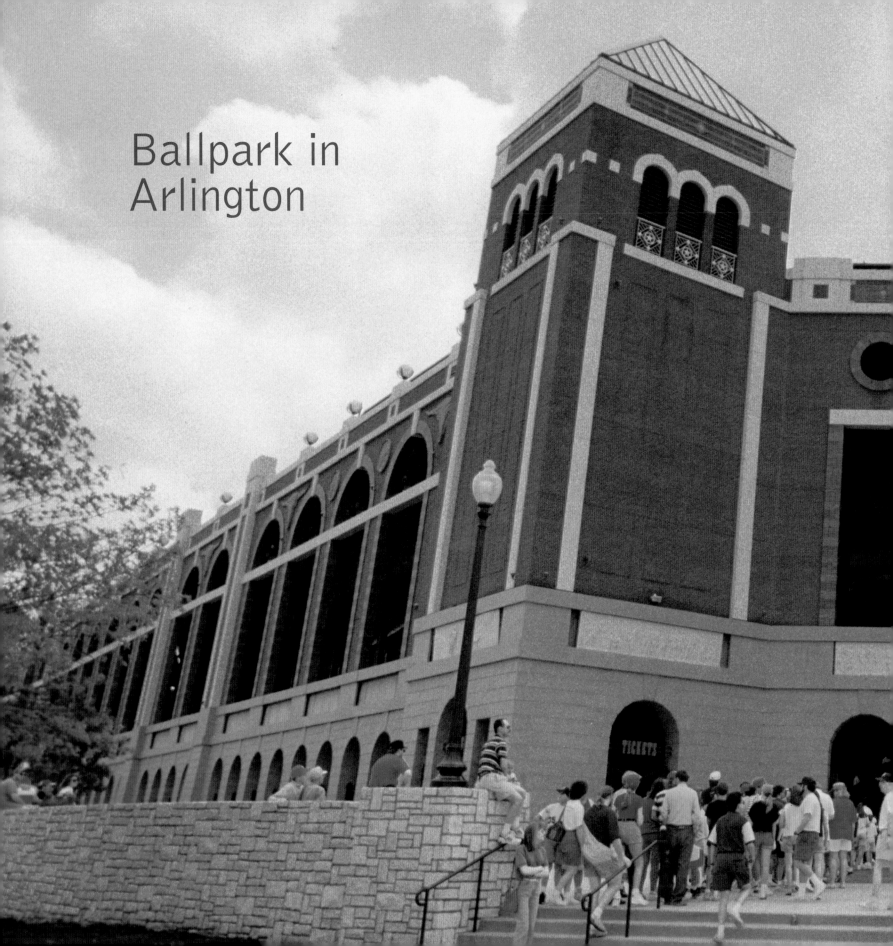

Ballpark in Arlington

MIKE PAGLIARULO
"Ballpark in Arlington is a great place to get ready to play a game: There are batting cages underneath the stands. The grass is better than the old Arlington Stadium, the background to see the ball is better, and the sound system is better. They have the restaurant in right field. You can sit down, watch a game—I would actually go to the restaurant after the game and watch how they cleaned up the field. One of the nicest things about it was the people down there, how warm they were to the players."

BRIAN MOEHLER "One of the more beautiful ballparks in baseball, it has a little bit of Tiger Stadium in the right-field bleachers, the way the stadium is set up outside with the brickwork. When you drive up to it you see the beauty of it, and once you get inside you see a little bit of each ballpark incorporated into the stadium."

BERT BLYLEVEN "It's a fantastic stadium. But I don't like it because I played in the old Arlington Stadium and this new ballpark really cuts down the wind. In the old ballpark, the wind used to blow in from right field; it was more of a pitcher's park. Now it's more of a hitter's type of ballpark."

HE TREND of ballpark construction in the 1990s continued here with the retro brick outer facade and the intimate, asymmetrical interior. For the most part, the architects achieved their goals, except for the totally enclosed design, which isolates the stadium from the surrounding community. Of course, Arlington, Texas, is not really a city anyway, in the sense of having a downtown area containing densely packed, high-rise buildings. It is a mostly residential and commercial sprawl connecting Dallas and Fort Worth. This ballpark replaced Arlington Stadium, located two blocks away, which was built in the sixties when the idea was to locate new stadiums in the suburbs, easily reached via highways.

Among the niceties here is an overhang in right field, modeled after the porch in old Tiger Stadium. A target for batters, a sign similar to the Abe Stark Win-a-Free-Suit sign in Ebbets Field, was erected 501 feet from home plate, a prodigious blast even in this era of record numbers of home runs. Beyond the center-field fence, alongside a promenade, is a large group of offices, probably the most striking visual aspect of this place, including an elaborate gift and memorabilia store. Unfortunately, the very size and number of these offices amounts to the enclosure of the stadium, which blocks the view of the environs.

A reality of producing additional revenue inside the newer stadiums is club seating, which features wait staff at seats. Instead of standing in long lines at concession stands or waiting in seats hoping for a hot-dog vendor to wander by, fans pay a big premium for more luxurious service. Architectural accommodation for this level of seating, though, usually entails a higher upper deck. Another possible downside is missing some of the action while placing one's lunch order.

- *Home of the Texas Rangers*
- *Arlington, Texas: East Randol Mill Road, Ballpark Way, Pennant Drive, and Copeland Road*
- *Built 1993*
- *Opening Day: April 1, 1993*
- *Cost: $191 Million*
- *Seating Capacity: 49,166*
- *Largest Crowd: 50,920 (All-Star Game, July 11, 1995)*
- *Replaced Arlington Stadium, 1993*

DIMENSIONS	LF	LCF	CF	RCF	RF
(1994)	332	390	400	381	325
(1999)	334	388	400	381	325

DEAN PALMER "When we opened Arlington, we flew from spring training. It was dark; we got in late one night. That's the first time any of us had really seen the stadium. We walked into the locker room, they showed us the way to the dugout, and I remember walking out and they had all the lights on. And just the sight of that beautiful ballpark lit up at night, I think everyone was in awe compared to the old ballpark. To go from the old Arlington Stadium to the Ballpark in Arlington was like night and day."

BILLY WILLIAMS "You're seeing a little bit of the Polo Grounds, you see a little of Tiger Stadium . . . the flavor of past years, the flavor of baseball parks."

Bank One Ballpark

OVER THE PAST COUPLE of generations, with so much more baseball being broadcast on national television, most fans see a ballpark for the first time via the tube. But without experiencing a ballpark's ambience in person, you can get a distorted sense of the place. A perfect example is Bank One, or "the Bob," as it is affectionately known to the local fans. When seen on the two-dimensional screen, it's an overly large, phonylooking attempt at retro; in person, though, this is actually a terrific ballpark and a great place to see a game.

Comedian Nick diPaolo once commented, "I didn't know Tempe was a quarter-mile from the sun." About ten minutes from that suburb, in downtown Phoenix, rose this marvelous stadium. The retractable-dome roof is closed most days in late morning to protect against the intense desert heat. Despite the supposed difference from the humid heat of Florida, it is oppressively hot in the Valley of the Sun. An announcement overheard from the press box at the start of a game: "First pitch 6:35, as advertised; game-time temperature 97 degrees—but *dry*." It was said with more than a little sarcasm.

The roof remains closed often enough to cause severe problems in maintaining the natural grass surface. The mottled appearance of the green field detracts only slightly, though, from an otherwise beautiful structure. The intricate steel girders that support the roof, which can and do result in a warehouse effect in many fixed-domed stadiums, are actually attractive here. This modern feel is

GREGG JEFFERIES "I think to this day it's my favorite field. It's one field that when it's closed you can see the ball great, and when it's open you see the ball great. . . . The angles are unbelievable. The field plays as good as any field you'll ever play on. The ball flies pretty good there, too. You look forward to playing there."

LUIS GONZALEZ "It's a unique ballpark. There's a swimming pool in right center field; we have a retractable roof that we open up before games if the weather's not too hot. We have a center-field area for kids to play—it's called the Clubhouse Zone. I think it's a fan-friendly ballpark and a fun place to go watch a game."

RON DAVIS "It's probably the most gorgeous ballpark I've been to, and I've been to about all of them. The only bad thing about it is, it's got too many TVs. People are watching the TV sets instead of watching the game. When the scoreboard's going 'Cheer!' ain't nobody in the stands to see it 'cause they're all drinking beer, getting a hot dog, or underneath the stands in the bar. It's a little bit too nice. People don't come to watch the game—it's more of a social event than a ball game."

My favorite stadium to hit in. You see the ball incredibly well, and the ball just jumps like a helicopter!

—ALEX RODRIGUEZ

tempered by a few old-time features such as the dirt path from the pitcher's mound to home plate and the pillars that are in play in deep center field, akin to the flagpoles found in bygone ballparks. Modern features include colorful mural panels above the outfield walls that open and close along with the dome, and a swimming pool located just beyond the right-center-field fence, where fans cavort during the game. At dusk, the desert sky is a spectacular backdrop to this modern design wonder.

- *Home of the Arizona Diamondbacks*
- *Phoenix, Arizona: Fourth Street, Jefferson Street, and Seventh Street*
- *Built 1998*
- *Opening Day: March 31, 1998*
- *Cost: $354 Million*
- *Seating Capacity: 48,500*
- *Largest Crowd: 49,584 (October 6, 1999, vs. New York Mets)*
- *Nickname: The Bob*

DIMENSIONS	LF	LCF	CF	RCF	RF
(1999)	328	376	402	376	335

Busch
Stadium

ST. LOUIS has always been one of the great baseball cities. From the Gas House Gang of the thirties to the World Championship teams of the sixties and seventies, the Cardinals have enjoyed tremendous support from the St. Louis fans. The second ballpark here, known as Busch Stadium (the first one, initially known as Sportsman's Park, was demolished in the sixties), although lumped by some into the cookie-cutter concrete-bowl category, is really a wonderful place to watch baseball.

This Busch Stadium started out in 1966 with a natural grass surface. Three years later the decision was made to convert the field to artificial turf. Management insisted that the reason was that because the Cards drew fans from a large geographic area, it wasn't fair to attract them from so far away only to have games postponed because of wet grounds. Theoretically, since standing water on artificial turf can be squeegeed off, fewer games would have to be postponed. Whitey Herzog's Cardinals of the early to mid-eighties actually took great advantage of the fast surface, assembling a team of solid, speedy hitters with outstanding defensive skills. Over the years, though, it became apparent that it rains comparatively little in St. Louis during baseball season. So in 1997 the

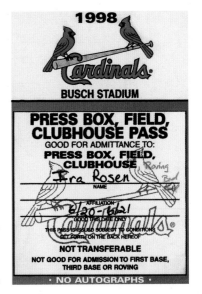

Cardinals removed the artificial turf and reinstalled natural grass. In addition, some seats were removed in the upper-right-field stands and a section was constructed to honor Cardinals Hall of Famers.

ALAN BENES "I think that the biggest excitement for me was the first time you actually step on the field as a player, knowing that you're here because you're going to be out on the field, not because you're going to sit in the seats and watch. It's an overwhelming feeling to be able to just come into the dugout, knowing that you're here because you're one of the players. You get the opportunity to go out and perform in front of thousands and thousands of people. The first time you actually put on the uniform to play in the first game . . . and the crowd sounds so loud compared to what you're used to. It's awesome."

ANDY BENES "The first stadium that I saw in professional baseball was Busch Stadium, back when I was in high school. We used to come over and sit in the upper deck and generally catch a weekend day game. And as a child, you always want to sit up as high as you can, so we thought it was pretty cool that we could sit up in the upper deck, even when there were seats available lower. So coming in high school and watching it, and then actually being able to play in it, was awesome."

JOE BUCK (BROADCASTER) "My earliest memory . . . is probably walking hand in hand with my dad down into the dugout here at Busch Stadium, and walking out and seeing the size of the field. . . . My earliest memory is not just of the ballpark but of the players. To see these athletes walking around and to know that this is their place, this is their office; whereas everybody else's day-to-day office is . . . a cubicle, or you strive for an office with windows. These offices throughout Major League Baseball are wide-open beautiful green fields with dirt, and what you're supposed to do is flop around, slide, dive, and throw a ball around. And I think you understand that at an early age at a ballpark, just by watching what's going on on the field before a game. And to see the guys watering the field, raking the dirt, guys out there throwing a baseball around—it's what every kid grows up dreaming about."

I'd been playing in the minor leagues, high school, Little League, and to see the perfection, almost a perfect setting—you know, the grass is green, it's level, the dirt is real manicured, it was like a dream. Busch Stadium. That's where I came up, right there.

— WILLIE MCGEE

Busch, built to accommodate the NFL's Cardinals as well as the Major League Baseball team, is on the large side. The football franchise moved to Arizona in the mid-nineties, and though a new football stadium was built to house the transplanted Los Angeles Rams, there has been no cry for a new baseball-only field here. Perhaps that can be attributed to the arrival in 1997 of Mark McGwire and his shattering of Roger Maris's home run record the following year. In this age of limited attention spans, there are few ballparks in which the fans focus as thoroughly as when McGwire comes to bat. In any event, the sea of red in the Busch stands—fans outfitted in all manner of Cardinal-red attire— attests to the great atmosphere of this aging but lovely ballpark.

- *Home of the St. Louis Cardinals*
- *St. Louis, Missouri: Stadium Plaza, Spruce Street, Walnut Street, and Broadway*
- *Built 1966*
- *Opening Day: May 12, 1966*
- *Seating Capacity: 49,275 (1966); 54,727 (1990); 49,676 (1998)*
- *Largest Crowd: 56,782 (October 14, 1996)*
- *Former Names: Civic Center Stadium, 1966; Busch Memorial Stadium, 1966–1983*
- *Former home of NFL's St. Louis Cardinals*

DIMENSIONS	LF	LCF	CF	RCF	RF
(1966)	330	386	414	386	330
(1992)	330	378	402	378	330

BERNARD GILKEY "I can remember the first day I got called up. I had been going to Busch Stadium since I was young, watching the games. And it was pretty memorable for me because I had the opportunity to play in my hometown in Busch Stadium. First day I got called up I played and there was about forty-some thousand, so it was pretty exciting for me, just seeing all the people, and I was just kind of in awe for the whole game."

MARVIN BENARD "I guess when they made Busch Stadium, Three Rivers, Riverfront, they almost look like the same three cookie cutters. But it was amazing what they did when they took out the turf and put a little paint job on that place. And to me, that's probably one of the best fields to play on. . . . The fans come out to the games, they love their team. It's also the place I got my first major-league hit."

BOB CARPENTER (BROADCASTER) "I do the Cardinals games along with doing ESPN. And doing the Cardinals games, that's my team. I grew up with them; it's a real thrill for me. But whenever we're on final approach to Lambert Field in St. Louis, we come across the Mississippi River and right off the left wing is the Gateway Arch and Busch Stadium. And there's that round cookie cutter down there with that beautiful grass sitting in the middle of it. And I look down into the ballpark and it just gives me a thrill every time I see the place. Because in a great baseball city like St. Louis, if you grew up there, you've got to be a baseball fan."

Camden Yards

AFTER THIRTY YEARS of constructing multipurpose stadiums, someone finally decided to build a baseball park. Camden Yards was the finest ballpark built in many generations, and it inspired other great facilities, including Coors Field and Jacobs Field. It is a wonderful blend of modern comfort with nostalgic touches, such as the upper-deck overhang reminiscent of Tiger Stadium and Ebbets Field, creating its own unique character.

With the proliferation of luxury boxes and the tendency to build larger stadiums to accommodate professional football, quite often baseball fans sitting upstairs do not get a passable view. Not so at Camden Yards, where there is scarcely a bad seat in the house. And unlike at older stadiums, the overhang does not block the view from the rear twenty rows of the lower deck. Other great features include the old B&O warehouse that looms large beyond the right-field wall, where the Orioles maintain offices; the vintage clock above the scoreboard in center field; the promenade of Eutaw Street just over the right-field fence; and the city skyline beyond center field. All contribute to a wonderful part-of-the-city atmosphere.

There is much debate about whether taxpayers should pay for sports stadiums that house professional teams owned by private investors. Advocates for the teams' owners insist that cities benefit from publicly financed stadiums both directly and intangibly in the form of civic pride. It has never been proven conclusively whether a city has increased its rev-

BRIAN JORDAN
"Camden Yards in Baltimore, my hometown—it's a great stadium. We played an exhibition game in spring training last year there. It was great being home and it was great playing in that park. I mean, it's a great park, and I think they began a tradition with the brick look, and Coors Field picked up on it and Jacobs Field. It's an excellent, excellent field."

DAVID DELLUCCI "My first major-league game I ever played in was in Camden Yards. I will never forget for the rest of my life, when they sing the national anthem and they get to the spot where they go, 'Oh!' . . . Sometimes when I hear the national anthem at other fields, I even go, 'Oh!' 'cause it's just stuck with me forever."

DON MATTINGLY "My favorite was Camden. I thought it was a great place to play. It felt like an old-time ballpark."

I think Camden Yards is the best stadium I've ever played in . . . You get 47,000 people every night to see a ballgame. Very exciting.

—HAROLD BAINES

enues by funding a new stadium as much as the ball club has by playing in it. But the overall improvement to the community at Baltimore's waterfront district, where Camden Yards was built, cannot be denied. The Orioles franchise also experienced a marked upturn during their first season there and have remained among baseball's big-market, big-spending teams ever since.

Finances and politics aside, it's satisfying to watch a game at Camden Yards. Writer Mary McGrory once said, "Baseball is what we were; football is what we've become." Sitting in Camden Yards reminds us of what it might have been like when the game was young.

- ◆ *Home of the Baltimore Orioles*

- ◆ *Baltimore, Maryland: Eutaw Street, West Camden Street, and Portland Street*

- ◆ *Built 1992*

- ◆ *Opening Day: April 6, 1992*

- ◆ *Cost: $105 Million*

- ◆ *Seating Capacity: 48,041 (1992); 48,262 (1998); 48,876 (2000)*

- ◆ *Largest Crowd: 48,974 (October 12, 1996)*

- ◆ *Formal Name: Oriole Park at Camden Yards*

DIMENSIONS	LF	LCF	CF	RCF	RF
(1992)	333	373	399	386	318
(1993)	333	364	410	373	318
(1999)	333	364	400	373	318

FRANK THOMAS

"There's a lot of good, new pretty ballparks now. Baltimore's my favorite."

Candlestick Park

BETTER KNOWN to Bay Area fans as "the Stick," this ballpark has been replaced by Pacific Bell Park, located in the China Basin section of downtown San Francisco. And not a moment too soon.

In 1957, Brooklyn Dodgers owner Walter O'Malley convinced New York Giants owner Horace Stoneham that his shrinking fan base and deteriorating ballpark necessitated a move west. The Dodgers had already cut a deal including stadium ownership with the city of Los Angeles to move from Brooklyn. The city of San Francisco promised to build a new ballpark to lure the Giants out of New York. The team played their first two seasons in an old minorleague park known as Seals Stadium.

Horace Stoneham flew to San Francisco to scout a site for the Giants' new

home. He was brought to Candlestick Point, a picturesque spot just inland from San Francisco Bay, adjacent to a major highway about fifteen minutes south of downtown San Francisco. At about 10:00 A.M., it is truly a beautiful place. So the deal was done, but the city

retained ownership of the stadium. Unfortunately, the light morning breeze off the bay turns into a steady piercing gale by midafternoon, rendering the point and the ballpark rather inhospitable. Perhaps Mr. Stoneham never visited the site at night and never heard the words of Mark Twain: "The coldest winter I ever spent was summer in San Francisco."

CHILI DAVIS "My first step into a Major League Baseball stadium was Candlestick Park. At the time, my first time in there, knowing that I was a part of the San Francisco Giants, I was in awe. I was in awe at not only the stadium but the fact that there were people watching me take BP. But then the awe went to 'Brrrr' 'cause it was cold."

PAUL KONERKO "I think the worst stadium I played in was Candlestick. It was just miserable. The weather was miserable. You'd have to walk all the way from the right-field foul pole to the third-base dugout if you were the visiting team. The wind's howling; nothing's really good about playing there. I'd hate to have been a home player and had to play all your home games there. That, and the fact that I got traded there and I had to walk across the field during a game while I got ousted from the Dodgers."

LARRY BOWA "I lived in Sacramento, and at that time the Giants were the closest big-league team, and I remember going [to Candlestick] watching games. . . . It was windy and cold, but it was something that I'll never forget, going there watching a game with my dad."

BOBBY J. JONES "I actually enjoyed pitching at Candlestick. I kind of enjoy cool weather—not too cold, but cool, comfortable. And I think a lot of it had to do with all my family being down to watch me pitch."

KIRT MANWARING "Candlestick, that's where I started my career. The old Candlestick, with the fog coming in and the wind changing. You never know what's going to happen from one inning to the next. A person has to play there every day, you try to tell yourself, 'Hey, we got an advantage.' But not really, 'cause we got to play eighty-seven games here and some teams only got to play ten games here."

Candlestick was once open in the outfield but was enclosed in 1971, mostly to add seats for the NFL's 49ers, but partly to diminish the effect of the wind. The enclosure did not accomplish the latter. And since the Giants rarely filled the 62,000 seats, the place had a cavernous, hollow feel. In addition to the constant ripping wind, a fog often rolled in off the bay, enveloping the ballpark like a cold, wet blanket. The few thousand loyal fans at most games tended to huddle together, wrapped in parkas and drinking coffee to stay warm. A gritty bunch.

One of the more famous stories about the Stick involves pitcher Stu Miller being blown off the mound during the 1961 All-Star Game. Actually, the story has been exaggerated: The wind merely caused Miller to sway a bit while he was in contact with the pitching rubber, with a runner on first base, causing a balk. This illustrates what the legacy of this stadium will be.

- *Former home of the San Francisco Giants*

- *San Francisco, California: Giants Way, Gilman Street, and Jamestown Avenue*

- *Built 1960*

- *Opening Day: April 12, 1960*

- *Final Game: September 30, 1999*

- *Cost: $1.5 Million*

- *Seating Capacity: 43,765 (1960); 59,091 (1991); 62,000 (1998)*

- *Largest Crowd: 62,084 (October 9, 1989)*

- *Known as 3Com Park, 1998–1999*

- *Nickname: The Stick*

- *Home of NFL's San Francisco 49ers*

- *Stadium enclosed 1971 (Cost: $416 Million)*

DIMENSIONS	LF	LCF	CF	RCF	RF
(1960)	330	397	420	397	330
(1991)	335	365	400	365	335
(1999)	335	365	400	365	328

JEFF BRANTLEY "First stadium I saw was Candlestick, and I was actually called up to the big leagues that day. It was the first time I had ever been to a big-league ball game. I was pretty nervous, to be honest with you . . . Real windy, but that day, could have been a tornado warning and I would have never known. I was just so encompassed by actually being in the big leagues, and being in a big-league park, that I really didn't notice the weather or anything else. All I knew was that the game was tied in the tenth inning and I was warming up, getting ready to go in, and we scored a run in the bottom of the tenth to actually win it. Flew to Atlanta the next day, and I played in my second big-league park and actually pitched in the game that day. So my first couple of big-league games were pretty nerve-racking."

JOE MORGAN "First stadium I saw was Candlestick Park. I went over and watched Willie Mays play after they had moved to the West Coast. And it just seemed like it was a beautiful place, and I just longed to be out there on the field."

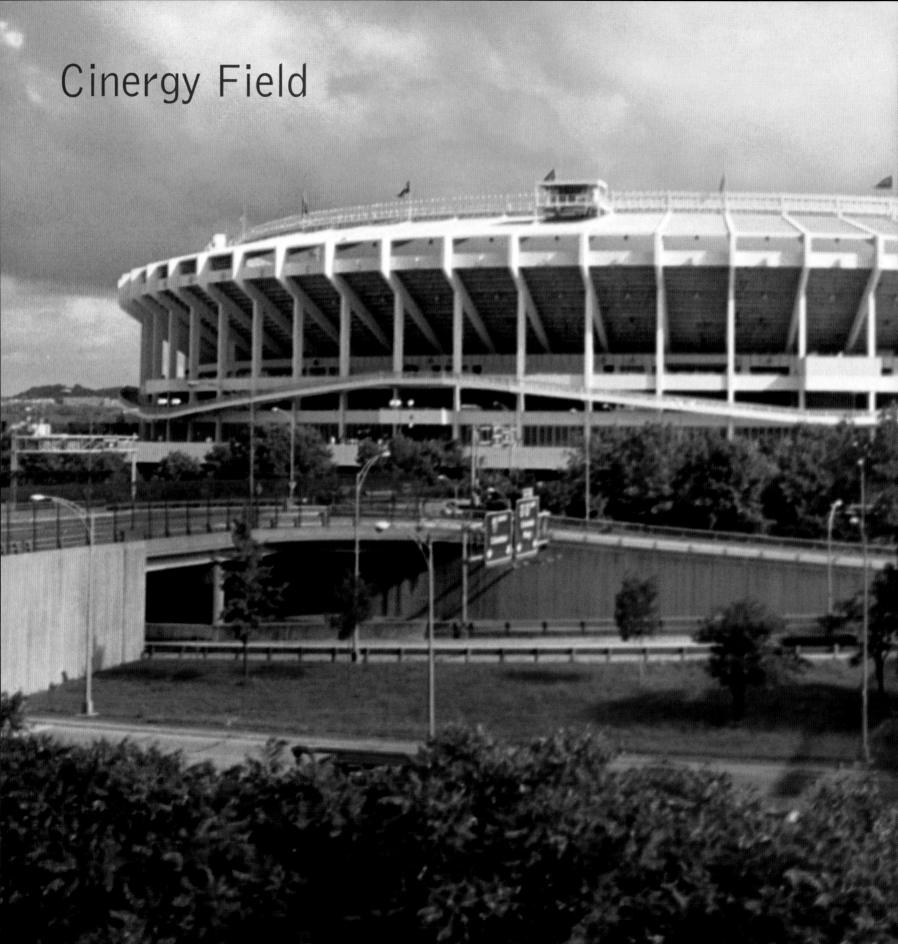

Cinergy Field

DWIGHT GOODEN "First time I saw a major-league ballpark was in '84 when I made the team [the Mets] my rookie year. And the first stadium I saw was Riverfront Stadium. And when I saw it, I was just amazed . . . You go back there three years later, it was like, 'Man, this is a small ballpark.' But the first time you see it, you're like, 'Wow, this is a big stadium and this is what it's all about.'"

DAVID JUSTICE "The first stadium I saw was Riverfront Stadium. I remember the electricity that was in the air. That was back during the Big Red Machine, probably back around '77, '78. And I remember it being exciting and big and just fun."

WILLIE BLAIR "First ball-park I saw was Riverfront Stadium, and I was pretty much in awe of it. I think I was only twelve or thirteen years old, and it was pretty special to be able to go out there and see all the guys that I'd watch on TV."

JAVY LOPEZ "The first time I saw a big-league stadium was when I first got called up in '92; it was the Cincinnati Reds. And when I got there, it was the most amazing thing I'd ever seen in my life. 'Cause I'd been playing in the minor leagues for six years before I came up to the big leagues, and I'd seen all different ballparks. And some of them, I thought they were pretty nice. But when I came to the big leagues, I saw a big difference, and I got very excited."

RIVERFRONT STADIUM

was the name until 1997 when, like many other sites in professional sports, naming rights to it were sold. So Cinergy Field it is.

Cincinnati was home to the very first professional baseball team, the Red Stockings, formed in 1869. Somewhere along the way, the word "stockings" took on a feminine connotation, so the name was changed to the Redlegs, then to simply the Reds. The oldest team in baseball plays in a multipurpose concrete bowl that also accommodated the NFL's Bengals. About the only nod to the Reds' long history is the use of old Crosley Field's home plate. But Reds fans will soon get a new baseball-only facility in the Queen City.

While there is nothing especially interesting about Cinergy Field, it was once notable as home to the only major-league dog, Schottsie, followed by his successor, Schottsie 02. These Saint Bernards, belonging to and named after former Reds owner Marge Schott, used to romp on the field alongside the players during batting practice. Occasionally, the big pooch would leave a deposit near second base. Two groundskeepers would dash out and clean up to the delight of dog and crowd alike. Inside this large, impersonal structure, amid the bright green artificial turf and with nary a glimpse of the city beyond, this was a welcome, if rather silly, diversion. In 1993, however, the National League banned the dog from the field, shortly after suspending Schottsie's owner.

The Reds continue to draw well here. But when this stadium is replaced, it remains to be seen whether this small-market team, unable to afford players the likes of whom formed the Big Red Machine in the seventies, will generate the revenue necessary to compete with big-market teams.

- ◆ *Home of the Cincinnati Reds*
- ◆ *Cincinnati, Ohio: Mehring Way, Second Street, Suspension Bridge Approach, and Pete Rose Way*
- ◆ *Built 1970*
- ◆ *Opening Day: June 30, 1970*
- ◆ *Seating Capacity: 52,392 (1970); 52,953 (1998)*
- ◆ *Largest Crowd: 56,393 (October 16, 1975)*
- ◆ *Former Name: Riverfront Stadium, 1970–1996*
- ◆ *Former home of NFL's Cincinnati Bengals*

DIMENSIONS	LF	LCF	CF	RCF	RF
(1991)	330	375	404	375	330

You watch TV and you see the parks, but there's nothing like it until you get on that mound. It's the greatest feeling in the world.

—ANDY ASHBY

Comerica Park

WHILE THE HOUSTON ASTROS moved from the spacious Astrodome to the intimate Enron Field, the Detroit Tigers left the homer-friendly Tiger Stadium for the expansive Comerica Park. The new playing field is the largest in the American League, bucking the trend of smallish new ballparks that began with Camden Yards in 1992. The Tigers experienced a difficult adjustment: Their long-ball hitters, who were used to reaching the fences at Tiger, found that they were no longer so close.

Though spacious inside, the external footprint of Comerica is quite small. The stadium is reminiscent of Frontier Field, a Triple A ballpark in Rochester, New York. Comerica is much bigger—with a seating capacity of 40,000 versus Frontier's 10,000 plus—but its location, a couple of blocks from the main downtown business district, its low-rise silhouette, and its brick facade and forest-green seats give the park a small-town aura—a pleasant change from the typical big-league experience.

The tremendous main scoreboard, flanked by two huge tigers, is the dominant feature. Unfortunately, the auxiliary scoreboard that posts the out-of-town scores has neither the charm of being hand-operated like the one in Enron Field nor the advantage of being large enough to display both leagues' scores at once. But the amenities here include a dirt path from the pitcher's mound to home plate, a

GREGG JEFFERIES "Driving up, I noticed what a wonderful job they did structurally. You get into the park, little things are really interesting: the angles in the outfield, the lights, the way they situated them. It's just a beautiful park, and it's a good hitter's park for a guy like me. But if you're a home-run guy, I don't know how much you care for it. There's definitely a lot of room."

DAMION EASLEY "Coming from Tiger Stadium, the mystique and tradition of Tiger, and coming into a brand-new park and starting a new tradition . . . It's spacious for a hitter, but at the same time it's good for line-drive hitters. There'll be some bloop singles that fall in. It's definitely unique in the fact that it's got a little bit of amusement for the kids with the Ferris wheel out there behind first base. You got the skyline in center field. Those are the things that, if you're a fan, you'll really appreciate in this stadium."

BOBBY MURCER "Comerica Park kind of went against the tradition of the way all the new ballparks are being built. It's a more spacious ballpark, lots of foul territory. When they're building the new ones, the fans are right on top of the field. They probably will have to make some adjustments—they've had a few complaints about how big the ballpark plays."

fountain in center field similar to the one in Kansas City's Kauffman Stadium, and an amusement area complete with Ferris wheel underneath the stands behind first base.

Early in Comerica's inaugural season, the Tigers did not draw sellout crowds, perhaps because of their awful start. But this gorgeous new ballpark is obviously only the beginning of the rebuilding of Detroit. A football stadium for the NFL's Lions will stand across the street from Comerica, and an $800-million office complex will open a couple of blocks away. With the ensuing retail establishments and, most important, downtown housing, Detroit hopes to replicate the success enjoyed by Baltimore and Cleveland—revitalizing a city around a centerpiece jewel of a baseball park.

- ◆ *Home of the Detroit Tigers*
- ◆ *Detroit, Michigan: Montcalm Street, Witherell Street, Adams Street, and Brush Street*
- ◆ *Built 2000*
- ◆ *Opening Day: April 11, 2000*
- ◆ *Cost: $260 Million*
- ◆ *Seating Capacity: 40,000*
- ◆ *Largest Crowd: 40,637 (July 16, 2000)*
- ◆ *Replaced Tiger Stadium, 2000*

DIMENSIONS	LF	LCF	CF	RCF	RF
(2000)	345	395	420	365	330

It plays pretty big.

We call it Comerica

National Park.

— BOBBY HIGGINSON

Comiskey Park (Old)

O N THE SOUTH SIDE of Chicago stood one of the great old ball-parks of America. But Comiskey Park, a victim of limited seating and crumbling infrastructure, was demolished in 1991. It is sorely missed.

Much was written in the eighties about the White Sox and Comiskey. When baseball moved into the television and free-agency era, it became paramount to increase revenues beyond ticket sales and concessions. One common source of additional income is a section of luxury boxes: small, well-furnished suites that are usually leased to corporations. During the 1982 remodeling of Comiskey to accommodate such boxes, serious structural flaws were discovered in the upper deck—not serious enough to prevent the Sox from playing there until 1990, but severe enough to greatly limit the number of boxes that could be built. The structural problems were also severe enough to cause several bitter years of lobbying, politicking, and threats by the team owners to move the team to Tampa–St. Petersburg. Finally, at the last minute in 1988, the Illinois state legislature came up with the money to build New Comiskey Park—right across the street from the old one.

In 1989, Comiskey Park, built in 1910, was the oldest stadium still in use in Major League Baseball, and it was a beautiful ballpark. It stood a couple of blocks from the Dan Ryan Expressway, a major high-way, and also a subway stop, called the El. The old-time look of the place created a feeling of warmth and intimacy, from the

My first game was

at Comiskey Park.

I had blinders on,

to tell you the truth.

I didn't know what

I was doing.

—JACK MCDOWELL

TOM MCCRAW "Old Comiskey Park was the first major-league park I ever played in. I came up with the White Sox in '63. The ballpark had a lot of nice things about it. It was a big ballpark, and we were a speed ball club at that time—we were line-drive hitters—so we liked that ballpark. We used to fix it up [for] every guy pitching: If Gary Peters was pitching, they fixed the mound different; if Joel Horlen was pitching, they fixed it different. You convert the ballpark to what your personnel were. That's the thing they don't do today."

AL KALINE "My memories of Old Comiskey Park are great memories, playing against the Chicago White Sox—the Go-Go Sox, Minoso, Rivera, Jim Landis, Sherm Lollar, Nellie Fox. Great teams, guys that would hit the ball, steal bases. As an outfielder, you always had to be ready to try to throw out somebody taking an extra base, 'cause they were certainly an aggressive team."

PETE MACKANIN "I was a kid in Chicago, went to Comiskey Park, sat in the left-field upper-deck bleachers, and couldn't believe where I was. And all I remember is the cigar smoke, smell of cigars."

◆ *Former home of the Chicago White Sox*

◆ *Chicago, Illinois: 35th Street, 34th Place, South Shields Avenue, and Wentworth Avenue*

◆ *Built 1910*

◆ *Opening Day: July 1, 1910*

◆ *Final Game: September 30, 1990*

◆ *Cost: $700,000*

◆ *Seating Capacity: 28,800 (1910); 46,552 (1927); 43,951 (1990)*

◆ *Largest Crowd: 55,555 (May 20, 1973)*

◆ *First All-Star Game in history played here July 6, 1933*

◆ *Major League Baseball's first exploding scoreboard installed, 1960*

◆ *Also known as White Sox Park, 1970s*

◆ *Demolished 1991*

DIMENSIONS	LF	LCF	CF	RCF	RF
(1910)	363	382	420	382	363
(1969)	335	370	400	370	335
(1990)	341	382	408	382	341

whitewashed brick on the outside to the exploding scoreboard on the inside. There were, of course, spots that looked run-down—in fact, a whole section of dilapidated seats in left field was actually closed off—but otherwise it did not seem like a park about to meet its demise.

In any ballpark, part of the charm (or lack of it) is the culinary fare. There was none better than at Old Comiskey. On field level behind home plate a cook stood over a sizzling barbecue grill, sweat pouring down from under a huge chef's hat, grilling burgers, steaks, and hot dogs to perfection.

The Sox wanted to bring something from the old park to the new one, so they brought over the infield dirt. They should have brought the chef and the grill.

HARRY KALAS (BROADCASTER) "My first time at a major-league ballpark was in 1946 at Comiskey Park, and it was a memorable one. The White Sox were to play the Washington Senators, and the field was covered because of rain. Because of the inclement weather my dad was able to buy box seats right behind the Washington dugout. There was no batting practice because of rain. We were in our seats behind the Senators' dugout and here was this ten-year-old kid, me, drinking in all the sights of this majestic stadium. A player, Mickey Vernon, poked his head out of the Washington dugout and saw this kid, me. He picked me up, took me into the dugout, introduced me to some of his teammates, and gave me a ball. Thus began my love of baseball and the Washington Senators, and eventually a broadcasting career in the game that I love. Oh, they did eventually play the game, but ten-year-old Harry didn't remember the score or even who won. He was on cloud nine. That day he officially became a baseball fan and a rabid supporter of the Washington Senators . . . The man responsible for my love of baseball, Mickey Vernon, lives in this area, and I see him from time to time, and I always thank him."

Friday night, June 30, 1989, was Seat Cushion Night. Standing in the upper deck, talking with an usher about the old park, the new park, and about what baseball meant to us, we felt a palpable sadness in the air. The field was empty and pristine, awaiting the start of the game. As the sun began to set, the fading light glinted off the old seats in right field. The seat cushion is long gone; the memory remains.

Comiskey Park (New)

DURING THE FINAL SEASON of play in Old Comiskey Park in 1990, the new stadium towered over the old one like a corporate monolith, diminishing the intimate, the comfortable, the past. As the 1991 season began in the new ballpark, corporations battled over the remains of Old Comiskey—people had discovered value in the seats, bricks, and detritus. The old ballpark still had not been razed five months into the season, as the White Sox and the wrecking company argued over who owned this material. The White Sox prevailed, the demolition proceeded, and there is now a parking lot where Old Comiskey once stood—as Joni Mitchell sang, "They paved paradise, put up a parking lot."

The main problems with New Comiskey are the elevation and the angle of the upper deck. There are two levels of club seats and luxury boxes above field level. But unlike all the other new stadiums built in the nineties, New Comiskey

does not allow for both these decks and a reasonable height to the upper deck. In fact, the first row of the upper deck in New Comiskey is farther from home plate than was the last row of the upper deck in Old Comiskey. And it isn't only the height that is disconcerting; it is the pitch, a steep gradation that makes watching a ball game from here an uncomfortable experience. Another problem is the location of this ballpark, in a run-down spot on the

I love New Comiskey.
It's a pitcher's park, and
it has the best infield in
the American League.

—KEVIN TAPANI

South Side. Although accessible to Chicago's elevated rail line, it does not feel connected to the city, and no effort was made to improve the surrounding neighborhood, as was done in Cleveland and Baltimore.

On the other hand, field-level box seats afford an outstanding view, and there is still an exploding scoreboard. And Sox pitchers seem to enjoy this ballpark for its spacious dimensions, as opposed to most of the other hitters' parks in the American League.

In 1991, prior to the opening of the new park, the hype led people to believe that this place would evoke Yankee Stadium. It does not. The only thing that New Comiskey has in common with Yankee Stadium is that the White Sox and Yankees are both in the American League.

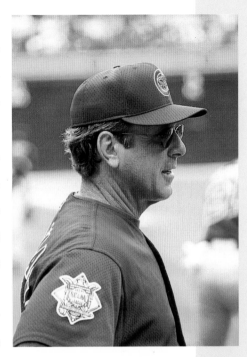

RENE LACHEMANN (COACH) "Everything is new in there, but it's not like a lot of the new parks. It seemed like it had very steep angles up on top. I guess the people are having problems with that."

JAMES BALDWIN "Chicago, Comiskey Park, was the first time I got to the big leagues to see a major-league stadium. That was very impressive, because when you look at the stadiums in the minor leagues, you look at maybe five to six thousand people. And when you get to a big-league ballpark, you see forty, fifty thousand. So that's a big jump."

RON SCHUELER "Contrary to all the things you hear about how steep it is, I think it's a great ballpark. I think it's very fair for pitchers. Hitting, you can get frustrated a little bit in April and September because of the winds. But to me, a very warm, friendly ballpark, and excellent for pitchers."

KEN HARRELSON "Comiskey Park is my favorite place to broadcast from. We have the best booth in baseball. A lot of people don't like it. They say that the upper deck is too steep. But the upper deck is no steeper there than it is in Texas, Cleveland, and any of these other places. If you put a plane on there and you've got the degrees of steepness, it'd be about the same."

◆ *Home of the Chicago White Sox*

◆ *Chicago, Illinois: West 35th Street, Wentworth Avenue, South Wells Street, and Stewart Avenue*

◆ *Built 1991*

◆ *Opening Day: April 18, 1991*

◆ *Seating Capacity: 44,321*

◆ *Largest Crowd: 46,246 (October 5, 1993)*

◆ *Uses exploding scoreboard similar to the one used in Old Comiskey Park*

◆ *Replaced Old Comiskey Park, 1991*

DIMENSIONS	LF	LCF	CF	RCF	RF
(1991)	347	383	400	383	347
(1999)	347	375	400	375	347

REGGIE JACKSON "First time I saw a Major League Baseball park I was in Philadelphia and I saw Shibe Park. That's Connie Mack Stadium. . . . And the first game I went to, Jackie Robinson was a player, he played second base. Duke Snider played center field. Jackie Robinson hit a home run right over my head. Left-field bleachers and all the blacks—well, colored, it was colored at that time—all the colored sat in left field. But I enjoyed myself. It was fifty cents to go to the ballpark. The grass was really pretty, the stadium was loud, it was beautiful. The ball sounded neat. They put water on the dirt in the middle of the game . . . It was great."

TOMMY LASORDA

"The first time I was in a major-league stadium was at Shibe Park in Philadelphia in about 1941. I was about fourteen years old. Well, I was in awe, after being from Norristown, Pennsylvania, never having seen a major-league ballpark."

KEN SINGLETON "In 1970, I got called up to the Mets, and one of the last series ever played in Connie Mack Stadium in Philadelphia was played by the Mets. And so I did get a chance to play in there for one series. The thing I remember about it is that I was very happy to hear they were going to have a new stadium in Philadelphia. And these days now they want an even newer one in Philly, they want to get rid of the Vet. But in those days, the locker rooms were very cramped. You could see a lot of history from the standpoint of an old relic, and it kind of looked like Ebbets Field but not as jazzed-up and certainly not in as good condition as I remember Ebbets Field when I was a kid. But [at] Connie Mack I remember seeing the Coke sign on the left-field roof where Dick Allen hit some balls up there, and it was a unique place. But I was glad the Vet came along."

Connie Mack Stadium

BEFORE THE PHILADELPHIA PHILLIES moved to the cavernous, multipurpose Veterans Stadium in 1971, they played in a bandbox of a ballpark known as Shibe Park, later renamed Connie Mack Stadium. As a young Mets fan growing up in the early sixties, my memories consist of the small black-and-white images that emanated from my twelve-inch television. In 1964, a rookie by the name of Richie Allen came up to the Phillies. Later known as Dick Allen, he had Hall of Fame potential but eventually earned the fans' wrath, perhaps for not fulfilling their expectations, and took to scratching out messages to his tormentors in the infield dirt. At the time, though, he was awesome. Owing to Allen's great strength (and the Mets' pathetic pitching), I can still see his blasts soaring over that left-field grandstand overhang, disappearing over the roof and into the night.

DIMENSIONS	LF	LCF	CF	RCF	RF
(1909)	360	393	447	393	360
(1969)	334	387	410	390	329

- *Former home of the Philadelphia Phillies*
- *Philadelphia, Pennsylvania: 21st Street, Somerset Street, 20th Street, and Lehigh Avenue*
- *Built 1909*
- *Opening Day: April 12, 1909*
- *Final Game: October 1, 1970*
- *Seating Capacity: 20,000 (1909); 33,500 (1925); 33,608 (1970)*
- *Largest Crowd: 40,720 (May 11, 1947)*
- *Originally known as Shibe Park, 1909–1953*
- *Home of the American League Philadelphia Athletics, 1909–1954*
- *Home of the National League Philadelphia Phillies, 1938–1970*
- *Replaced by Veterans Stadium, 1971*
- *Demolished 1976*

ROBIN ROBERTS "[My first time was] Connie Mack Stadium in Philadelphia, when the Phillies called me to the majors. The park was beautiful. I pitched that night—lost 2–0."

GENE GARBER "As a farm boy growing up listening to the Phillies on the radio, it was a great thrill to see my first game at Connie Mack as a twelve-year-old. The scoreboard clock and catwalk, 447 feet to center, the pillars, all still vivid in my mind."

Coors
Field

GEOGRAPHICALLY, THE MOVE by the Colorado Rockies from Mile High Stadium to Coors Field was only across town, but the new ballpark is worlds away in style and substance. In the continuing tradition of new retro ballparks such as Camden Yards, Coors is a beautiful, comfortable facility.

Fans granted the Rockies a sort of immunity during their inaugural 1993 season at Mile High, but by their third year in the National League, fans expected a winner and greeted sloppy play or poor pitching with loud booing. This was reminiscent of Mets fans at the Polo Grounds in 1962, indulging their Amazins with patience during a horrendous season; but with the Mets' move to Shea Stadium in 1964, fans' contentment with the lovable losers wore thin. So, too, the Rockies now face the win-now mentality at Coors.

The expanse of lush green outfield grass is stunning here, more so than at most major-league fields. Since Denver is situated over 5,200 feet above sea level—indeed, it is the Mile High City—the air is thinner, so the baseball travels farther. The fences are commensurately farther from home plate, creating more outfield space. From the Rockies' inception, they assembled teams long on power—the team nickname for a time was the Blake Street Bombers. But after falling to last place in 1999, team management decided to replace the power-hitting lineup with faster, more defense-oriented players, the better to cover the outfield gaps, which are enormous.

The sight lines at Coors are wonderful, from both the lower level and the upper deck. The outfield features a bleacher section called the Rockpile, and although the view from those seats is distant at best, the price of a ticket is extraordinarily low.

While not situated to encompass a panorama of downtown Denver, Coors still feels connected to the downtown area. A number of restaurants, brewery pubs, and souvenir shops sprang up when the ballpark opened, revitalizing a previously run-down area. And the outfield view does include, in the distance, the Rocky Mountains—one of the more beautiful vistas at a Major League Baseball stadium.

My favorite place to play in my short career is Colorado's Coors Field. It's nice to hit; you see the ball pretty well. The ball carries a lot—there's a lot of room to get hits.

—JAY PAYTON

QUINTON MCCRACKEN "My first experience in a major-league park was Coors Field, and when I walked out of the dugout, what startled me was the enormity of the park. It seemed like the parameters were endless. It's a very spacious field, it's green, it's a beautiful ballpark. It's like 400, 415 dead center and 330 down the lines, but foul line to foul line, it's just extremely large. And I was caught up in it, I was in awe. Looking up in the seats, it seemed like this place was almost the center of the universe."

CRAIG BIGGIO "It's beautiful being outside and being out there. It's just a healthy atmosphere to be there. They've got great people there, great fans—it's just a lot of fun."

RYAN THOMPSON "Coors Field is quite amazing. We opened that ballpark with the Mets in 1995. It would be a great place for any hitter. The ball flies there, it's a great atmosphere, good fans. It's a beautiful place."

◆ *Home of the Colorado Rockies*

◆ *Denver, Colorado: Twentieth Street, Blake Street, I-25, and Park Avenue*

◆ *Built 1995*

◆ *Opening Day: April 26, 1995*

◆ *Cost: $215 Million*

◆ *Seating Capacity: 50,200 (1995); 50,381 (2000)*

◆ *Largest Crowd: 51,267 (All-Star Game, July 7, 1998)*

◆ *Replaced Mile High Stadium, 1995*

DIMENSIONS	LF	LCF	CF	RCF	RF
(1999)	347	390	415	375	350

County Stadium

DUANE KUIPER "The first park I'd ever seen a major-league game in, I'll never forget. It was between the Cardinals and the Milwaukee Braves. It was the home of Aaron and Mathews, two guys I absolutely idolized as a kid. The thing I remember most, and I still look at it through the eyes of a kid, was that everything was so green. The other thing I remember is walking through the parking lot to the stadium and thinking that this place has to be absolutely huge because they're major-league players . . . So when I walked in, I expected it to be like the Grand Canyon, and it turned out that it was at least small. However, not small enough: When I played I didn't hit a home run."

OZZIE GUILLEN "You come from the country I come from, other kids never had the opportunity to do that. I was a lucky guy to come down to the big leagues and come to a big-league stadium, it's something you always dream or you're always looking for, especially when you sign. I think when you're in the major leagues, there's no ugly stadium—every one looks good. First stadium was Milwaukee Brewers, that was my opening day. County Stadium . . . It was to me the best ballpark I'd ever seen, because it was my first major-league stadium."

SCOTT BROSIUS "I never saw a big-league game growing up. The first big-league game I ever saw, I was actually playing in the minor leagues at the time. We went over and we played on Milwaukee's field after Milwaukee played that day. . . . At the time, I thought that was the greatest thing in the world, you know, Milwaukee County Stadium, all the seats and the scoreboard and all that. Once you get to the big leagues, you realize that was probably down on the list as far as the nicer parks around. But at the time it sure seemed like the best field I'd ever played on."

LARRY ANDERSEN "Going from the clubhouse through the tunnel, up the steps, and to step out onto the field and just look around, you're in awe, it's incredible."

MILLER PARK replaced Milwaukee's County Stadium in 2001. Although the degree of decay was not as apparent at County as it was in Old Comiskey and Arlington, this ballpark nevertheless joined the ranks of the extinct. County served the people of Milwaukee since 1952, initially as the home of the National League Braves. Fans do not support the Brewers as they once did—the franchise has enjoyed only mild success here since the move from Seattle in 1970, appearing in only one World Series in 1982. It is hoped that the new stadium will boost attendance.

County was the first ballpark built with suburban commuters in mind, located several miles from downtown and accessible by car. Having a stadium near the highway enabled fans to arrive early and tailgate, an activity normally associated with football. Fans often arrived hours before game time, setting up grills and picnic tables in the parking lots, filling the air with rich aromas. There was nothing else like it in baseball. Since the new ballpark is adjacent to the old one, hopefully this tradition will continue.

County Stadium, like Memorial in Baltimore, is a solid-looking brick structure. There are steel support beams in every section, holding up the roof and giving the ballpark an old-time feel. But with the overhang of the upper deck, the last twenty rows of the lower deck have limited visibility. On the other hand, there are few bad seats in the upper deck, and the bleachers are terrific.

Along with beer, Milwaukee is known for its wonderful sausage—or brats, short for bratwurst. Part of the American ballpark experience is the hot dog, the frank, the red hot; but by any other name, it is simply not a Milwaukee brat. Savoring this finest of stadium cuisine, sitting under the brilliant blue Wisconsin sky, is a reminder of why we love baseball.

- *Former home of the Milwaukee Brewers*
- *Milwaukee, Wisconsin: Blue Mountain Road, Harnischfeger Road, and I-94*
- *Built 1953*
- *Opening Day: April 14, 1953*
- *Final game: September 28, 2000*
- *Cost: $5 Million*
- *Seating Capacity: 36,011 (1953); 53,319 (1991); 53,192 (1999)*
- *Largest Crowd: 56,562 (October 17, 1982)*
- *Former home of the National League Milwaukee Braves, 1953–1965*
- *Replaced by Miller Park, 2001*

DIMENSIONS	LF	LCF	CF	RCF	RF
(1953)	320	376	404	376	320
(1992)	315	362	402	362	315

BILLY SAMPLE "In 1978, five days before the end of the Triple A season, I was informed by manager Rich Donnelly that I was going up to the majors for the first time. The call-ups had to share space with each other in this old wooden clubhouse. The outfield bleachers and grandstands that greeted me as I exited the tunnel to the dugout were just as old. Yet it was definitely major league, in spite of the unaesthetic beauty of the dull grays, oranges, and greens, the predominant colors of the twilight setting. That orange hue of twilight was behind Jerry Augustine as he delivered the game's first pitch: a low, knee-high sinking fastball on the outside part of the plate, which I promptly lined in a moderately hard fashion into right center field for a base hit."

> *The first stadium*
> *I saw in the big leagues*
> *was Crosley Field in*
> *Cincinnati . . . It was*
> *an old ballpark, but to*
> *me it was brand new.*
> **—TONY PEREZ**

Crosley Field

ALTHOUGH NOT HIGHLY REGARDED in its time, Crosley's influence is still being felt more than thirty years after its final game. Houston's Enron Field features an incline in deep center field, an homage to the Terrace, a unique and rather steep incline in Crosley's outfield. It was difficult to discern on my small television, but radio announcers would frequently describe this anomaly as outfielders lost their balance (and the baseball) trying to negotiate the hill. A constant factor in games, Enron's terrace, which also contains a flagpole in play, is a mere gimmick by comparison.

- Former home of the Cincinnati Reds, 1890–1970
- Cincinnati, Ohio: Findlay Street, Western Avenue, and York Street
- Built 1884
- Opening Day: May 1, 1884 (American Association)
- Final Game: June 24, 1970
- Seating Capacity: 25,000 (1912); 33,000 (1938); 29,604 (1964)
- Largest Crowd: 40,720 (May 11, 1947)
- Originally known as Cincinnati Base Ball Park, 1884–1889
- Also known as Western Avenue Grounds, 1891; League Park, 1892–1901; Palace of the Fans, 1901–1911; Redland Field, 1912–1933
- Replaced by Riverfront Stadium (now Cinergy Field), 1970
- Demolished 1976

DIMENSIONS	LF	LCF	CF	RCF	RF
(1912)	360	380	420	N/A	360
(1958)	328	380	387	383	366

PAUL O'NEILL "The first field I saw, I was four or five years old, my mom and dad took me down to Crosley Field in Cincinnati. I grew up in Columbus, and we saw [the Reds] play the Pirates, and we sat right behind Roberto Clemente, I remember that. And as a little kid, you look at those stadiums like it's . . . a summer vacation, just driving down to Cincinnati and watching a Major League Baseball game."

DON ZIMMER "The first major-league park I saw was Crosley Field. It was a unique park, small, a park that I'll always remember. And I loved playing there. I guess being an old-timer, I still like parks like Crosley Field, Wrigley Field, Fenway Park—they're still my favorite parks."

JIM BROSNAN (FORMER PITCHER, AUTHOR) "I grew up in Cincinnati. When I was eight years old I was taken to Crosley Field and thought it was lush baseball paradise. Sixteen years later I pitched for the Cubs in what I distinctly remember as a nasty little bandbox of a ballpark."

JOE NUXHALL "My first visit to Crosley Field, I was in awe of the size of the stands and the green grass on the playing field."

Dodger Stadium

CALLED CHAVEZ RAVINE while it hosted both the National League Dodgers and the American League Angels in the early sixties, Dodger Stadium is one of the few ballparks built before 1980 that is not on the endangered list. Though showing a little wear and tear in spots, it remains a clean, comfortable place despite the acrid smog that occasionally settles in.

The Dodgers franchise still retains a nostalgic aura despite the team's recent upheaval: its sale and the firing of two managers in the same year. This type of turnover is not uncommon for some teams, but from 1954 until 1994, the Dodgers had only two managers—Walter Alston and Tommy Lasorda.

Although they arrived from Brooklyn as recently as 1958, the Dodgers are the West Coast equivalent of the Yankees, an institution—perhaps in part due to the rivalry the teams shared in New York. These two teams met in seven World Series during the forties and fifties, with the Dodgers winning only once, in 1955. They have met in the Series three more times since the move. No two teams have played for the World Championship as often as these two, and their names will be forever linked in baseball history.

Chavez Ravine, the area where Dodger Stadium stands, is near downtown Los Angeles. The land was deeded to the Dodgers by the city, and this is one of the few team-owned ballparks in baseball. It is a credit to the Dodger organization that the ballpark is maintained so well.

Much appreciated are the sonorous voice of the public-address announcer and the organ music played between innings, as opposed to the loud rock-and-roll atmosphere at some stadiums. Most of the seats afford a decent if not fabulous view of the game, except in the top deck. Once you ascend to these

VIN SCULLY (BROADCASTER) "The biggest thing about Dodger Stadium to me is the beauty both inside and outside the ballpark. They spent a lot of money on landscaping, and of course we have the mountains. It's the best scenic view, I think, in all of baseball. And when the nights are reasonably clear, as you look out toward center field it looks for all the world like a Frederic Remington painting. It's a jewel of a place."

PEDRO MARTINEZ "Dodger Stadium was the first one I went to see. It was great. The impression was the biggest, the biggest you could ever have . . . because these stadiums, you don't have them in the minor leagues. My rookie year, at the end of the year, I went to see my brother, Ramon. So when I went, they were almost going to the playoffs, and there were a *lot* of people."

OZZIE SMITH "I grew up in Los Angeles, so going to Chavez Ravine was always an exciting time for me, because it was the home of the Dodgers and the mystique that went along with the Dodgers—Koufax, Drysdale. That was it."

PAUL OLDEN (BROADCASTER) "My most enduring recollection is of Dodger Stadium, 'cause I grew up there, literally. I sold programs there, I sat in the stands and did play-by-play, practicing my skills there. So I knew every inch of that ballpark because I was there for every game for eight or nine years in a row. And just the overall beauty and serenity of Dodger Stadium— it's a very peaceful place, especially when you're there early and no one's in the stadium except the ballplayers on the field and those of us who were preparing to go to work."

TRAVIS LEE "It was Dodger Stadium. We had seats behind the dugout . . . You go out there and see the green grass, the brown dirt, smell of hot dogs. Like everyone says, it all came true when I was about five years old."

- *Home of the Los Angeles Dodgers*
- *Los Angeles, California: Pasadena Freeway, Elysian Park Avenue, Scott Road, and Solano Canyon Road (park encircled by Stadium Way)*
- *Built 1962*
- *Opening Day: April 10, 1962*
- *Cost: $23 Million*
- *Seating Capacity: 56,000*
- *Largest Crowd: 56,242 (October 24, 1981)*
- *Formerly known as Chavez Ravine, 1962–1965*
- *Former home of the American League Los Angeles Angels, 1962–1965*

DIMENSIONS	LF	LCF	CF	RCF	RF
(1962)	330	380	410	380	330
(1991)	330	370	400	370	330
(1999)	330	385	395	385	330

nosebleed seats, there is no exit except out of the ballpark, which prevents wandering to other levels.

The notorious southern California smog is usually in evidence, and since the stadium is in a ravine, the air doesn't circulate as well as it does in San Diego and Anaheim. So maybe it's respiratory congestion and not the infamous traffic jams that prompt fans to leave in the seventh inning.

I still remember the day—I mean, I don't know the exact date, but I remember the day I walked into the stands and sat down and watched the game with my dad.

—JASON GIAMBI

LARRY WALKER "When I was a kid, I lived in Vancouver. We'd go to California for vacation and I saw games at Dodger Stadium. I remember sitting in this big, humongous arena—and remember, I'm Canadian, I didn't watch baseball, didn't grow up with it, so it was really new to me. And the one thing for some reason I remember about it the most is sitting in the second deck, and it was opening day, and all I remember was paper airplanes flying by me and all over the place, onto the field. And I couldn't figure out what was going on. I had no idea why this was happening. Now here I am in the big leagues, and it always seems that when you do an opening day or the last game of the season, people want to throw things on the field; and that seems to stick in my mind, seeing these paper airplanes flying by my head all the time and toilet-paper rolls coming out of the sky. So it was something different that I'd had no idea about, and now I know *all* about it."

AL MARTIN "I got a chill, I just can't believe the field looked like it did. I was probably nine or ten, going up to see the Dodgers play. It was a day I'll remember forever."

BILL RUSSELL "I remember playing in Bakersfield in 1968, coming here as a nineteen-year-old, and the team was on the road, and walking out here, standing on the mound, looking around, [I] said, 'Wow, this is bigger than my hometown.'"

REGGIE SMITH "I was here when they opened Dodger Stadium, and I was a sixteen-year-old kid in awe. The dimensions of the fence and the fact that you're seeing the stands and coming in and looking at the people in the stands from the left-field area, it was an awesome experience."

MATT WILLIAMS "It was Dodger Stadium, 1987. Completely in awe. I grew up watching the Dodgers, watching Ron Cey, Steve Garvey, Davey Lopes, guys like that. Finally got a chance to be there. I was twenty-one years old and scared to death. I was a huge Dodger fan, so it was a thrill to watch a game there. And it was even more of a thrill to play there."

DARRYL STRAWBERRY "As a child growing up . . . I always wanted to play in the major leagues. Just to see Dodger Stadium, to see that stadium and to see the grass, how beautiful it was, the infield and the ballpark—I just thought it was a dream that came true."

ROYCE CLAYTON "Dodger Stadium became like my home, because growing up I attended a lot of games, and I think I've sat in every section all the way down to the field box, 'cause my dad knew somebody who worked for the Dodgers, knew Jim Gilliam. So by the time I was to my mid-teens, I had basically run over every little nook and cranny in Dodger Stadium, to the maintenance room—just couldn't make it down to the field or the dugout. The thing I remember most is just wanting to touch my feet on the dirt and just seeing how close I was, and I could feel it. In my high school, we played a championship game there . . . unfortunately, we lost the game. But I swore to myself that I'd be back . . . to Dodger Stadium to play a game in the big leagues."

BRAD FULLMER "Dodger Stadium. I live in L.A., about twenty minutes from here. This is the place I grew up coming to . . . I always sat right up there with my parents, came for years . . . It's weird to be playing here now."

RYAN KLESKO "I think my first experience was to go to Dodger Stadium when I was real little. My mom and my dad and my family and some kids from Little League . . . just beautiful Dodger Stadium, packed house, one of the umpires walked over and handed me a ball down the third-base line. I think I was probably about seven or eight years old, so baseball fit in my life right away after that. When I got drafted, when Atlanta came to town, I worked out at Dodger Stadium . . . I took batting practice on the field and hit some balls out with a wooden bat, signed with the Braves the next day. I was out there early, saw a lot of the guys out there early, hitting. Zane Smith and Fernando Valenzuela pitched that night. I was right behind home plate, and Dale Murphy walked up and shook my hand."

TONY LARUSSA "I just signed a contract as a seventeen-year-old out of high school and the Kansas City A's flew me to L.A. to work out for a week with the major-league team, so it would have been Dodger Stadium. I think that's where the Angels were playing at the time, if I'm not mistaken: Chavez Ravine. And I was impressed with the beauty, the spaciousness, the luxury of the clubhouse, everything that you attach to the major leagues. It was about what you expected, and more."

Ebbets
Field

I GREW UP in the New York metropolitan area, and my biggest baseball regret is not having seen Ebbets Field. Everyone in my small world in the fifties was a Yankees fan. Since there wasn't interleague play back then, the Yanks and the Brooklyn Dodgers, playing in different leagues, did not meet during the regular season. Occasionally, they would play an exhibition game for charity. But for the most part, Yankees fans had no reason to visit Ebbets. In fact, I don't recall anybody being even remotely interested in the National League, so certainly no one would have cared to venture to Brooklyn just to see the ballpark. In retrospect it seems shortsighted, but there was no nostalgia for lost ballparks in the fifties.

Part of the charm for Dodgers fans was living in the same neighborhood as the ballpark. The stadium was part of their culture, much as Wrigley Field is to Chicagoans. Perhaps even more important was that many of the players also lived in the neighborhood. Fans felt connected to their heroes. Those players who lived in another part of the borough would often take the subway to games. The closeness that the fans shared with Dem Bums, along with the close proximity of players to fans once they were inside the cozy ballpark, has contributed to the mystique of the Dodgers and Ebbets Field.

CHARLIE STEINER (BROADCASTER) "Ebbets Field, 1957. The most vivid memory I have, and I think about it all the time. Because in those days, there was no color television, it was black-and-white. You had Happy Felton's Knothole Gang down the right-field line. And I remember my father holding my hand, walking into Ebbets Field, and walking down the ramp, and suddenly the sun was shining and there was really green grass. And it wasn't gray! And all the signs on the left-field bleachers, and then the Schaefer scoreboard down the right-field line was all in color. It was like I'd arrived in the Land of Oz. It was one of the single most astonishing moments of my life. I was seven years old, and I can remember it as vividly today as it was forty-two years ago."

GEORGE CARLIN (COMEDIAN) "It was Ebbets Field and I took the subway by myself—I was about nine—out to Brooklyn, got off the BMT, got off at the Franklin Avenue station, and walked to Ebbets Field. It was a Yankees-Dodgers Easter Sunday exhibition game. And it was great. I don't remember the score, I'm sure the Dodgers lost; I was a Dodgers fan. In Ebbets Field . . . it was working class and wasn't like Yankee Stadium. It was real people with smelly armpits, and they were great people, and you felt them close to you because the stadium was so intimate."

My favorite memory was in Ebbets Field. We beat the Bums the last day of the 1950 season to clinch the pennant. After the last out, I had such a feeling of relief and satisfaction.

— ROBIN ROBERTS

The first game I played for the Dodgers in Ebbets Field in 1944, I had never heard noise like that. It was beautiful.

— GENE MAUCH

KEN SINGLETON "The first time I saw [a game], I was five years old. My dad took me to Ebbets Field to see the Dodgers play the Philadelphia Phillies in a doubleheader. . . . We had a television set, I watched just about all the games I could. But our TV set was black-and-white, and the first time I walked up the tunnel and looked at the greenness of the grass—and the people who can remember Ebbets Field, the outfield signs on the walls were just vivid color. The guys on the field in those days were Jackie Robinson, Duke Snider, Pee Wee Reese, and Don Newcombe, and those were the guys who made me interested in the game. Gil Hodges, I don't want to leave him out, Roy Campanella—these are the guys who made it look easy. And once I turned pro and got to the major leagues, I realized that it wasn't easy."

MAURY ALLEN (AUTHOR) "The first time I saw the inside of Ebbets Field I cried. My father and older brother made me walk up the steps to my bleacher seat in left field. I was five. I cried again over the Dodgers when Bobby Thomson homered. I was eighteen. My first memory of significance was when I slept on the street on the corner of Bedford Avenue and Sullivan Place in 1947 to get a World Series bleacher ticket. Rex Barney pitched and Joe DiMaggio homered. It is over thirty years now since the closing, and I still miss Ebbets Field."

PHIL PEPE (AUTHOR) "Nothing could compare with my first sighting of Ebbets Field. I was six years old at the time, and my uncle and cousin took me to a game. I had been following the Dodgers on the radio and had the benefit of Red Barber's descriptions, not only of the action on the field but of the ballpark and its surroundings. That, plus a book with a diagram and dimensions of every major-league ballpark, helped me feel like I was right there when I was listening to a Dodgers game.

"We lived in the Gravesend section of Brooklyn, about five miles north of Coney Island. To get to Ebbets Field we would take the Culver Line elevated train to Coney Island, where we would change to the Brighton Beach line, which took us to the Prospect Park stop, about a thirty-five-minute ride in all. Upon exiting from the subway station and arriving on the street, the first sight I saw was the huge Bond bread sign atop the bakery. From there, it would be about a ten-minute walk to Ebbets Field, past Prospect Park and the trolley terminal. Ten minutes that seemed like hours. We'd turn a corner—and I can still picture this—there rising above, seemingly to the sky, was the ballpark's huge rotunda, above which was the name Ebbets Field. Just the sight of that sign made my little boy's heart leap with joy, excitement, and anticipation. To this day I still get chills thinking about it.

"Inside the ballpark, the field was the greenest green. The uniforms of the home team were the whitest white, the chalk lines of the batter's box

- *Former home of the Brooklyn Dodgers*
- *Brooklyn, New York: Bedford Avenue, Montgomery Street, McKeever Place, and Sullivan Place*
- *Built 1913*
- *Opening Day: April 9, 1913*
- *Final Game: September 24, 1957*
- *Seating Capacity: 18,000 (1913); 35,000 (1937); 31,902 (1952)*
- *Largest Crowd: 41,209 (May 30, 1934)*
- *Site of first night game ever played: June 15, 1938*
- *Demolished 1960*

DIMENSIONS	LF	LCF	CF	RCF	RF
(1913)	419	N/A	477	N/A	301
(1957)	348	351	393	352	297

My first glimpse of a major-league stadium was Ebbets Field, July 15, 1955. I pitched a complete-game victory, 3–1, against the Cincinnati Reds. Yes, the first major-league game I'd ever seen.

—ROGER CRAIG

and foul lines were so neat and precise, and the players, my heroes—Duke, Jackie, Campy, Pee Wee, Gil, and Newk—were bigger than life; baseball cards come to life before my very eyes. Ebbets Field was so quaint, so intimate, so close to the action, you could hear the players and coaches shouting, and you felt you could almost reach out and touch them. Even the bleacher seats, sixty cents, where I spent many an afternoon, were a treat. I remember the double-decked stands in left field and center field, the high cyclone fence atop the scoreboard in right field that protected the homes across the street on Bedford Avenue, and the Abe Stark Clothing Store sign beneath the scoreboard that said, 'Hit Sign Win Suit.' I doubt anybody ever did hit that sign. They say Ebbets Field was more than a ballpark; it was a state of mind, a way of life. When the Dodgers left Brooklyn and Ebbets Field was torn down to make room for a housing project, it was as if my youth had vanished. But all these years later, more than a half century, Ebbets Field still lives in my mind and heart."

ERNIE HARWELL (BROADCASTER) "On August 4, 1948, I broadcast my first big-league game—Dodgers versus Cubs at Ebbets Field. Jackie Robinson stole home [in the] first inning. Russ Meyer, the Cubs pitcher, protested, cursed, and was tossed out of the game. Profanity and obscenity went over our airwaves. Dodgers went on to win."

MARK CONNORS (COACH) "I believe I was maybe six or seven, 1955, 1956. Ebbets Field, my dad took me to a ball game there. That was the first ball game I ever saw. The first impression that I recall is walking in and seeing the green grass, how green everything seemed to be. I'll never forget—Don Newcombe pitched against Joe Nuxhall, I think it was the Cincinnati Reds. After that, I saw the Polo Grounds, Yankee Stadium. But Ebbets was my first big-league ballpark and it will always be in a corner of my mind when I think about my first major-league game and going there with my dad. I remember where we sat."

MARTY APPEL (AUTHOR) "My father was born in Brooklyn in 1916, and I was born there in 1948, so you would think my first trip to Ebbets Field would have been a rite of passage. But as it happened, it was my father's first game as well. We went in 1954—I have no recollection of the date or the opponent. In fact, I remember only two things: the slivers of green as you walked up the ramps, finally unfolding as the massive green outfield, and the sight of Roy Campanella catching. Our seats were behind the screen, pretty far up and off to the first-base side, but to my young eyes, Campy was great fun to watch, being so round and hustling all the time. I'm sure latter-day kids of seven got the same feeling of entertainment watching Kirby Puckett.

"I wasn't hooked—my recollections of baseball really begin with the '55 World Series—but I do know I was at that game, my only time in Ebbets Field. I wish I had more memories of Ebbets, but I'm glad I was there at least once.

"I have heard the Dodgers no longer play there."

Edison International Field

ADAM KENNEDY "I don't know if I'd rather have any other stadium to go to every day than Edison. If you didn't have a smile on your face, you'd have a smile come BP time, 'cause everything about it is so great."

TREVOR HOFFMAN "First memory of going into a ball field would be Anaheim Stadium back in the eighties. My dad was an usher there, and I'd go in to work with them, and he'd take us in early to go through the ushers' section and then up to his section. It was pretty neat 'cause we'd park outside of the left-field wall, actually beyond the stadium, and you'd walk through and walk underneath the big *A* when it was out in left field over there before they enclosed it."

JARET WRIGHT "When I was growing up, my father played. So my first time, I was actually inside Anaheim Stadium. It was a great experience. I was real young; I was a baby. Since then I've seen my share of them, and every single one of them has something special."

BEN GRIEVE "I like those rocks out there. This is probably the nicest one we've been in all year. Playing surface is real nice, it's got a good atmosphere with the fountains out there and everything. Good weather. I like this place a lot."

#40	CALIFORNIA Angels.
	THURSDAY
208	JUL 04,1991 VS.
2	6:00 PM KANSAS CITY
	FIREWORKS
117	UPPER VIEW
	$7.00 90798
	GAME TIME SUBJECT TO CHANGE • NO REFUNDS OR EXCHANGE

ORIGINALLY KNOWN as Anaheim Stadium, naming rights caused the ballpark's change of name. Though also victim to football-dictated expansion in 1989 (increasing seating capacity from 43,550 to 64,593), happily the stadium was reconfigured back to a baseball-only facility in 1998, with capacity scaled back to a reasonable 45,050. It is now among the more enjoyable ballparks in baseball.

Edison Field is located along what surely must be the busiest family-entertainment street in the country, Katella Avenue. Located here are Disneyland and Knott's Berry Farm as well as dozens of motels and restaurants. Despite the congestion, the city has managed to maintain a family atmosphere. The ballpark, too, is a clean, friendly attraction.

The previous owner, Gene Autry, was beloved by players and fans, and his memory remains strong here. The Angels never won a pennant during Autry's tenure, but he inspired a loyalty rarely found between baseball players and management. Though he passed away in 1998, his spirit is not forgotten. Among the giant murals of famous Angels pictured along the outfield fence is the smiling cowboy's face.

Before the stadium was enclosed, it featured what was then the largest freestanding scoreboard in the country, topped by the Angels logo, a huge *A* encircled by a halo. When the ballpark was enclosed, the *A* was replaced by a smaller *A* visible beyond left center field. During the earthquake of 1994, this smaller *A* crashed into the upper deck, causing considerable damage. Unfortunately, even though the stadium was reconfigured, the big *A* was not returned to its place. But the rocks and waterfalls beyond the center-field fence add visual interest and set this place apart from the other California ballparks.

My first thought was "How'd they get the grass mowed like that, to make the little pattern in the grass?"

—DARRYL KILE

- ◆ *Home of the Anaheim Angels*
- ◆ *Anaheim, California: Katella Avenue, State College Boulevard, Orangewood Avenue, and Orange Freeway*
- ◆ *Built 1966*
- ◆ *Opening Day: April 19, 1966*
- ◆ *Cost: $24 Million*
- ◆ *Renovation Cost (1997–1999): $100 Million*
- ◆ *Seating Capacity: 43,500 (1966); 64,593 (1989); 45,050 (1998)*
- ◆ *Largest Crowd: 64,406 (October 5, 1982)*
- ◆ *Formerly known as Anaheim Stadium*
- ◆ *Old Nickname: The Big A*
- ◆ *New Nickname: The Big Ed*
- ◆ *Former home of NFL's Los Angeles Rams*

DIMENSIONS	LF	LCF	CF	RCF	RF
(1966)	333	375	406	375	333
(1991)	330	386	404	386	330
(2000)	330	386	408	386	330

Fenway
Park

FENWAY USED TO BE WELL-KNOWN for the Curse of the Bambino: When Red Sox owner Harry Frazee sold Babe Ruth to the New York Yankees in 1920 to help finance his theatrical play, he supposedly doomed the franchise to perpetual failure. While the Sox didn't win a World Series for 86 long years starting in 1918, that curse was broken with their spectacular win in 2004. The fans here are a loud, passionate bunch, and they kept rooting for their team throughout their long dry spell.

If Wrigley Field is the most beautiful ballpark, Fenway may be the most vibrant. Nowhere in baseball is the rooting more fervent than here on Lansdowne Street. Boston's college-town aspect probably contributes to the frat-party atmosphere, which starts several blocks from Fenway at the T station. There is a sense of neighborhood here, with food and souvenir vendors, ticket scalpers, and anxious fans all moving about quickly, noisily. There are surely more taverns outside the immediate environs of Fenway than at any other ballpark in the big leagues, perhaps fueling the fire.

Fenway is one of the tougher tickets in baseball, especially when the arch-rival Yankees are in town. Since the seating capacity is only 34,000, the demand is often greater than the supply. But a half hour or so before game time, the ticket window offers obstructed-view seats. Old parks like Fenway were built with steel posts to support the upper deck, and seats behind these posts have an

obstructed view—not the best way to watch a ball game. The seats that are not situated behind the columns, however, offer some of the best sight lines

It's my favorite park, that's where I met my wife—right behind the Green Monster.

—DANTE BICHETTE

- Home of the Boston Red Sox
- Boston, Massachusetts: Lansdowne Street, Yawkey Way, Ipswich Street, and Van Ness Street
- Built 1912
- Opening Day: April 20, 1912
- Seating Capacity: 27,000 (1912); 34,171 (1991); 34,218 (1999); 33,871 (2000)
- Largest Crowd: 47,627 (September 22, 1935)
- Famous for the Green Monster left-field wall—37 feet high, plus 23-foot screen, erected 1936; advertising signs removed, wall painted green 1947
- Also known for huge Citgo sign visible over the Green Monster, erected 1965

DIMENSIONS	LF	LCF	CF	RCF	RF
(1912)	321	N/A	488	N/A	313
(1991)	315	379	420	380	302
(1999)	310	390	420	380	302

WHITEY FORD "My first major-league game was in Fenway Park, July 1950. I went in the game about the fifth inning; we were losing 10–0 at the time. Two innings later I was out of the game, losing 17–4. I never saw a park with such a short left-field fence. I thought I'd be back in the minors the next day. The Red Sox lineup was DiMaggio, Pesky, Dropo, Williams, Stephens, Doerr, Goodman, and Tebbetts—real tough hitters except for Birdie Tebbetts. Luckily I learned to pitch to them for the next seventeen years!"

MO VAUGHN "When I had gone up from Triple A to the big leagues, the first time I jumped in Fenway Park . . . I just knew that this is the big leagues, this is what it's all about, what you work for all your life."

LOU PINIELLA "I've always enjoyed Fenway, although it's outdated now. But it's got a lot of history and a lot of tradition. I like the Green Monster, the closeness of the fans to the playing area. And it only seats thirty-five or thirty-six thousand people, so it's full, which is always fun."

JACK BUCK (BROADCASTER) "Well, I lived in Massachusetts and I was ten years old in 1934 and I saw Fenway Park. I thought it was the biggest building I'd ever seen in my life."

JIM RICE "I was a line-drive hitter. I liked to play in New York; I liked to play in Detroit. And of course, playing the wall in Fenway Park, a lot of my line drives were just singles, maybe doubles. In any of the other ballparks, they'd have been out."

DAVEY LOPES "I was about ten years old and my most vivid memory was saying, 'One day I'm going to play in this ballpark.'"

JERRY REMY "The most amazing thing to me was when I was a kid, going to Fenway for the first time. That's where I saw my first major-league game and, of course, back in those days, there was no color TV, it was just starting to come in. And to walk into Fenway Park—first you see the lights as you're driving up the highway, every light you see you think is Fenway. Finally, you get to see the light standards, so you know you're close. Then, walking in the stadium and seeing the green grass and the green of the big wall out in left field, that's something that will always stay with me."

DARIN ERSTAD "I just remember walking in there and the smell will always stay with me. You could just tell it was a ballpark by the smell. It smelled of hot dogs."

in baseball: The view from the left-field corner, in most parks a distant vantage at best, is remarkably close to the field; the tiny upper deck is closer to the action than at any other big-league park; and although the bleachers in center and right field are comparatively far removed, the fans who gather here for the atmosphere don't seem to mind.

The most notable feature in Fenway—perhaps the most memorable detail of any ballpark—is the Green Monster outfield fence, which stretches from the left-field foul line to left center. This wall—37 feet high with a 23-foot screen above it—beckons both left-handed and right-handed hitters while causing pitchers to lose sleep. It can turn an ordinary pop fly into an adventure. The most famous of these was Bucky Dent's 1978 "can of corn" home run off Mike Torrez, which helped the Yankees defeat the Red Sox in a one-game playoff to

It was 1937. I was with Joe Cronin, and we were back of third base up in the stands. He said, "This is where you're going to play your career."

— BOBBY DOERR

decide the American League Eastern Division Championship.

The wall is indeed a monster, but it wasn't always green. Prior to 1946, it was covered with advertisements, but the ads were removed and lights were added when the park was renovated for the 1947 season. Fans arriving early often head for the third-base side to marvel at this imposing structure. The Green Monster has an outer layer of tin, replete with thousands of dents from the baseballs bouncing off it; batting practice is thus punctuated with pings. The sound isn't the same on television.

Fenway Park is now the oldest ballpark in baseball. The areas underneath the stands are cramped, and when several hundred standing-room-only fans combine with high humidity on a midsummer's day, it can make for a steamy, crowded experience. But it is one that should not be missed, for there is talk of building a new stadium in Boston. No matter the design, a new ballpark could never duplicate the Fenway experience.

Forbes Field

ARRIVING AT MOST BALLPARKS a couple of hours early affords one the opportunity to watch batting practice. A large portable cage is set up behind home plate, and batters scurry in and out, taking rips at soft tosses from the coaches, getting loose before the game. About forty-five minutes before game time, the cage is removed and stored out of the way, beneath the stands. But at Forbes, the center-field wall was so far from home plate that the cage was simply rolled out to the wall and left on the playing field during the game. Legend has it that few batted balls ever made it as far as the cage.

The most famous home run in baseball history is Bobby Thomson's Shot Heard 'Round the World in the 1951 National League playoff game between the Giants and the Dodgers. Arguably the second most famous homer occurred in 1960 at Forbes: Bill Mazeroski's World Series–winning blast for the Pittsburgh Pirates off the New York Yankees' Ralph Terry. Who hasn't seen the footage of Yogi Berra running back to the left-field wall, then veering back toward the infield in case the ball hit the wall and bounced back? This was followed by Mazeroski rounding third base and heading home while mobbed by his teammates. Relatively few people witnessed that event in person, but none of the millions of fans who have seen footage of it will forget Forbes Field.

GEORGE WILL (AUTHOR, COLUMNIST) "My first memory is Forbes Field in 1950. My father was a minister in Donora, Pennsylvania, the home of Stan Musial, where Ken Griffey Jr. was born, as a matter of fact. And we went to the ballpark and we were playing the hit song of the day, which was 'Goodnight, Irene.' The Pirates, who didn't beat many people that year, beat the Cardinals 9–0, and a guy named Wally Westlake hit a grand slam home run. I remember the people in the stands, good ethnic crowd eating lots of peppers. And I remember going around and seeing a young broadcaster as he prepared to work named Harry Caray who was doing the Cardinals' broadcast then for the Griesedick Brothers Baseball Network. I'd just turned nine."

STEVE BLASS "I got called up from Triple A. I drove in the rain from Columbus up to Pittsburgh and went immediately to Forbes Field. I had been there as an eighteen-year-old, trying out the day I graduated from high school, and I really was totally intimidated and really didn't do much. But when I was called up to play in the big leagues, it was an absolute thrill. I always remember going into the clubhouse, and the clubhouse manager took me over and said, 'This is your locker, son.' And I stood there and he said, 'Well, why don't you put the uniform on, go out and walk out.' And I said, 'Well, it's raining.' And he took me by the arm and he says, 'You see, there's three uniforms in there. If that one you're going to put on gets wet, we've got two more just like it. And that's why they call it the big leagues.'"

FRANK THOMAS (THE ORIGINAL ONE) "When I first walked in I saw how big it was and the players from the stands looked small. The grass was green and plush. I said, 'That is where I want to play when I get old enough.' And you know, I had my dream come true. I played in Forbes Field with the Pirates."

VERN LAW "The day I arrived was an exciting day—I had never seen such a big park with so many tiers of seats in my life. So it was kind of overwhelming for a young man who never saw more than a couple hundred people at a game on a high school and sandlot level."

ART HOWE "I was a youngster in Pittsburgh, Pennsylvania, and Forbes Field was the first major-league field I ever saw. The thing I remember when I was very young and I went to a game at Forbes Field was that in those days they let you walk out through center field to leave the ballpark. Schenley Park was out beyond the fence in center field, and I remember walking out to the warning track, it was like 460-some feet to straightaway center there. And it used to actually have the batting cage in center field during the game. I turned around, and I could not see home plate from there. It seemed like there was a hill between me and home plate, and I couldn't believe how huge the ballpark was."

◆ *Former home of the Pittsburgh Pirates*

◆ *Pittsburgh, Pennsylvania: Boquet Street, Sennott Street, and Schenley Park*

◆ *Built 1909*

◆ *Opening Day: June 30, 1909*

◆ *Final Game: June 28, 1970*

◆ *Cost: $2 Million*

◆ *Seating Capacity: 23,000 (1909); 41,000 (1925); 35,000 (1960)*

◆ *Largest Crowd: 44,932 (September 23, 1956)*

◆ *Replaced by Three Rivers Stadium, 1970*

◆ *Demolished 1971*

DIMENSIONS	LF	LCF	CF	RCF	RF
(1909)	360	457	435	416	376
(1954)	365	406	435	408	300

RALPH KINER "Forbes Field, 1946. After opening the season in St. Louis, I arrived in Pittsburgh by train at about 10:00 A.M. The city was like midnight from the heavy smoke from the steel mills. We had a workout scheduled that afternoon. I walked into the ballpark and took a look at the playing field for the first time and was appalled: 365 feet down the left-field line and then a scoreboard that extended high above the outfield fence. And then in center field the distance number was 456 feet. It was so deep they parked the batting cage there. I couldn't believe this was my new home. I wanted to telephone the scout who signed me, Hollis Thurston—how could he have done this to me?"

DEL CRANDALL "I was raised in California, so I didn't see a major-league stadium until I played in a game in the major leagues or at least joined a major-league team. And that was in Pittsburgh, I was with the Boston Braves at that time. And when I walked in, I think the thing that struck me the most was the immensity of it . . . I'd come out of a Class B league, as we had in those days to join the major-league club. And I think it was just the fact that 'My goodness, how do you ever hit a ball out of here?' and 'How do you ever hear yourself think?'"

Fulton County Stadium

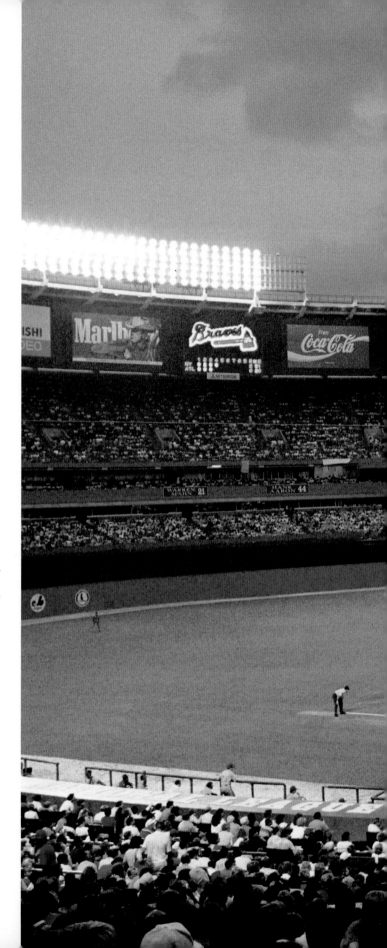

T HE BRAVES MOVED from Boston to Milwaukee in 1953, then to Atlanta in 1966. Each move saw the team increase attendance at first, followed by a decline as the novelty wore off. By the late eighties, despite the broadcast of games on the WTBS Superstation, the Braves were drawing poorly at home, the result of consistently bad play over a very long period of time. Bad trades, worse free-agent signings, and an unproductive farm system resulted in last-place finishes and were reflected in a tattered ballpark. The hiring of Bobby Cox, first as GM, then as field manager, reversed the team's fortunes. As the Braves climbed in the standings, so did their attendance. Ballparks come alive only when filled with happy, excited fans.

Before it was demolished in 1997, replaced by Turner Field across the street, this ballpark was lumped together with the other so-called cookie-cutter stadiums built in the sixties and seventies: Pittsburgh, Philadelphia, St. Louis, and Cincinnati all played in multipurpose plastic-and-concrete bowls. The difference was that the Atlanta Braves played on natural grass. While a minority of infielders enjoy playing on artificial turf because of the predictable bounce of ground balls, most players much prefer playing on real grass. The vast majority of fans also like to see the game played on natural grass. Fortunately, all stadiums currently under construction or in the planning stages will feature grass.

From the outside, Fulton County Stadium did look similar to all the other cookie cutters. Situated adjacent to Route 75, a mile or two from downtown Atlanta, it continued the trend started by Milwaukee in the fifties of building ballparks with suburban commuters in mind. Unlike Milwaukee County Stadium, however, it was also built with the NFL in mind, which accounted for its circular sameness, the symmetrical dimensions, and an overly large feel.

CHIPPER JONES "I think the first time I saw [a major-league ballpark] I was thirteen, up here in Atlanta, Fulton County Stadium. It was one of the most beautiful things I'd ever seen. . . . [At my first game in the majors] I couldn't feel my legs, couldn't feel my arms. When I got a pinch hit appearance against the Cincinnati Reds, I was so excited I think if the guy had thrown one off the backstop, I would have swung at it. But I made contact: It was a swinging bunt down the third-base line. I beat it out for a base hit. The only reason I probably beat it out was 'cause my adrenaline was pumping so hard."

My first experience was Atlanta Braves stadium when I was just probably eight or nine years old. Hank Aaron hitting, I think it was number 709 . . . That's something that kind of sticks out.

—**TURNER WARD**

The improvement of the infield surface here coincided with the 1991 signing of first baseman Sid Bream and third baseman Terry Pendleton, tightening the Braves' defense and boosting the young pitching staff led by Tom Glavine and Steve Avery. It was around this time that the country became aware of the fans' notorious tomahawk-chop chant, repeated often, loudly, and for the most part without prompting from the PA system. Political correctness aside, it got the crowd excited and helped revive a moribund ballpark. In fact, the fans were so involved that they forgot to do the wave.

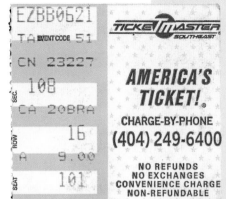

BUCK SHOWALTER "The first [ballpark] I ever saw . . . in the big leagues was in Atlanta—Fulton County Stadium. Couldn't imagine any place like that."

JOHN FRANCO "My first was Atlanta Fulton Stadium . . . Compared to the Little League fields I played on, it was a blessing. Used to playing with big rocks, big holes, stuff like that, so nice clean green grass and nice clean stadiums—it was a blessing."

BILLY TAYLOR "My first memory of a major-league game was . . . I'd say I was probably about eleven years old up in Atlanta, watching the Braves play the Dodgers [at] Fulton County Stadium, and that's back when they had Chief Nokohoma, and I got an autograph from Tommy Lasorda. I still have that baseball . . . That's the first major-league game I ever went to."

TODD GREENE "The first time I saw a big-league stadium was when I was about ten years old, when I went to the Braves stadium. I said, 'Wow!'"

- *Former home of the Atlanta Braves*
- *Atlanta, Georgia: Fulton Street, Georgia Avenue, Capitol Avenue, and Pullman Street*
- *Built 1965*
- *Opening Day: April 12, 1966*
- *Final Game: October 24, 1996*
- *Cost: $18 Million*
- *Seating Capacity: 51,500 (1965); 52,007 (1990)*
- *Largest Crowd: 53,775 (April 8, 1974)*
- *Known as Atlanta Stadium, 1965–1974*
- *Nickname: The Launching Pad*
- *Home of the International League Atlanta Crackers, 1965*
- *Former home of NFL's Atlanta Falcons*
- *Replaced by Turner Field, 1997*
- *Demolished 1997*

DIMENSIONS	LF	LCF	CF	RCF	RF
(1966)	325	385	402	385	325
(1991)	330	385	402	385	330

Jacobs Field

SIMILAR IN SIZE and design to Camden Yards in Baltimore, the Jake (named after former Indians owner Richard Jacobs) is not only a wonderful ballpark but it was instrumental in reviving a decayed section of downtown Cleveland. Perhaps more important, it gave folks here a renewed sense of civic pride after decades of hearing slurs about their city. Within a complex that includes an upscale shopping mall as well as the indoor Gund Arena, Jacobs Field is the centerpiece of a now vibrant downtown area.

Municipal Stadium, home to the Indians for six decades prior to 1994, was close to Lake Erie and was often a victim of lake-effect weather. Jacobs Field, located several blocks inland, is not immune to the same elements. But most days, the wind doesn't whip off the water as it once did at the Mistake by the Lake.

Seating at Jacobs Field is marvelous on the lower level and in the upper deck, even with the two tiers of luxury seating. Unfortunately, procuring a ticket for any game is a problem for those who do not hold season tickets, as the Indians have sold out virtually every game since the ballpark opened. With a much smaller seating capacity and infinitely better sight lines and facilities than the old stadium, this success is not surprising in a town with such a long baseball history. Of course, fielding a perennial pennant contender doesn't hurt either. Some of the overflow crowd can view the game standing in the left-field pavilion above the wall, comparatively close to the action due to the short distance from home plate.

There has been much speculation about the rapid increase in home runs in the major leagues. The juiced-up baseball, the watered-down pitching staffs,

MIKE SIROTKA "It's exciting to see the turn-around that Cleveland in general has had with its sports teams. Before Jacobs Field came into existence, it was a very dull, dreary stadium-type atmosphere. And now it's one of the most exciting parks in baseball, especially with the Indians

being a competitive team year in and year out. You go to the ballpark, you know you're playing one of the best teams in baseball, and that's one of the primary reasons you play this game—to compete against the best and hopefully have success against the best. The ballpark is very beautiful, great fans, and it's really a pleasure to play in."

JACK CURRY (COLUMNIST, *NEW YORK TIMES*) "The reason I think Jacobs Field is such a good ballpark is because it was such an improvement over what the Indians had at Municipal Stadium. Even if they had twenty thousand people on a cold night in Cleveland, it felt like the place was empty. They became a contender, they moved them into this new ballpark, and it was like Cleveland became a different city. Everyone rallied around the team and the ballpark. I always get the feeling when I'm at Jacobs Field that the people there are having fun."

MIKE BORDICK "When Jacobs Field came in, people were pretty excited about that. Municipal didn't draw too well. The new park in Cleveland, they pack the place every night. Plus, it's got all the modern conveniences. I think it's a pretty legitimate park."

and the hitters' increased weight training are among the explanations given for this. But a prime reason must be the opening in recent years of smaller ballparks like Jacobs Field. These so-called bandboxes not only provide a cozier setting for viewing the game but also definitely contribute to the big fly effect.

KENNY LOFTON "Jacobs Field is the favorite stadium that I play at. Coming from the old stadium, it's something different."

KEN HARRELSON "There's no question in my mind: I think the prettiest stadium in baseball is Jacobs Field. I love it."

ROBIN VENTURA "Having played in Municipal Stadium, the switch to Jacobs Field has really changed their whole team outlook. They have more of a home-field advantage. It's a nice ballpark even as a visitor. It has a feeling of an older ballpark, because of the noise of the crowd, the way it goes back and forth across the stadium."

- ◆ *Home of the Cleveland Indians*
- ◆ *Cleveland, Ohio: East Huron Road, Broadway, Ontario Avenue, East Ninth Street, and Carnegie Avenue*
- ◆ *Built 1994*
- ◆ *Opening Day: April 4, 1994*
- ◆ *Cost: $175 Million*
- ◆ *Seating Capacity: 43,345 (1994); 42,865 (2000)*
- ◆ *Largest Crowd: 44,280 (October 5, 1996)*
- ◆ *Nickname: The Jake*
- ◆ *Replaced Cleveland Municipal Stadium, 1994*

DIMENSIONS	LF	LCF	CF	RCF	RF
(1994)	325	368	400	375	325
(1999)	325	370	405	375	325

Jarry Park

WHEN DESCRIBING ballpark experiences, hardly anyone mentions the public-address announcers. Other than Bob Sheppard, a veteran of fifty-plus years at Yankee Stadium, these unsung fixtures of the game are for the most part nameless. This is true of the original PA announcer for the Expos at Jarry Park. His voice, however, will live on. This fellow took great pleasure in building up a dramatic introduction for a player in both French and English, then calling out the name with a flourish, specifically with two original Expos in 1969—Coco Laboy and John Boccabella. Their names will live forever for those who heard them in the ballpark or over the airwaves: CoooCoooCoooo Laaaa-Boooyyyy! John Booooooc-a-bellllllaaaaa!

There was a swimming pool beyond Jarry's right-field fence, and although it was not inside the stadium, the pool predates the one in Bank One Ballpark in Phoenix by thirty years. Parc Jarry, unlike most other obsolete ballparks, has not been demolished. It is still in use by the citizens of Montreal for amateur ball games and civic events.

DIMENSIONS	LF	LCF	CF	RCF	RF
(1969)	340	368	415	368	340

BOB MURPHY (BROADCASTER) "Jarry Park was kind of fun. Little minor-league ballpark, not even a *good* minor-league ballpark. Fans in the early part of the year would sit out on snowbanks and watch the game."

RON SANTO "Once in Jarry Park, Gene Mauch was the manager there, and he had told his pitcher to throw at me. I stepped out of the box and told Mauch if the pitcher threw at me, I was coming after him. So the pitcher threw pretty close to me, and I went in the dugout after Mauch, but I went in alone. Luckily, Dick Radatz, who was a friend of mine, grabbed me, so I wouldn't get the s—t kicked out of me."

JOHN VUKOVICH "I came up with the Phillies. My first big-league game was in Montreal—Jarry Park, Parc Jarry. It was cold."

BILLY WILLIAMS "Played in Jarry Park, which was a park that they played in before they got the new stadium. It had a swimming pool in right field."

◆ *Former home of the Montreal Expos*
◆ *Montreal, Canada: Rue Faillon, Rue St. Laurent, Rue Jarry, and Canadian Pacific Railroad*
◆ *Built 1968*
◆ *Opening Day: April 14, 1969*
◆ *Final Game: September 26, 1976*
◆ *Seating Capacity: 28,456 (1969)*
◆ *Largest Crowd: 34,331 (September 15, 1973)*
◆ *Known in Canada as Parc Jarry*
◆ *Replaced by Olympic Stadium, 1977*

97

Kauffman Stadium

THE KANSAS CITY ROYALS played their first four seasons in Municipal Stadium, for many years the home of the old Kansas City Athletics. In 1973 the Royals moved here, to what was then called Royals Stadium. For twenty-three years, the stadium, one of the better places to watch a major-league game, was covered with an artificial surface. In 1996, the turf was replaced with natural grass, turning a fine facility into one of the top five ballparks in baseball.

The only drawback to Kauffman is its location, virtually in the middle of nowhere. Built during the era of suburban stadium construction, it is a good distance from downtown Kansas City, with no sense of connection to the city. This could barely be called suburbia; rural would be a better description. The setting, though distant, is lovely, located amid grass and trees, situated in the Harry S Truman Sports Complex adjacent to Arrowhead Stadium, home of the NFL's Chiefs. Inside, the ballpark is intimate, with wonderful sight lines and a fan-friendly atmosphere.

Probably the best-known feature is the waterfall behind the outfield wall; the cascade of water can be seen throughout the game. Spanning the distance from center field to right field, the waterfall measures 322 feet across and is said to be the world's largest privately funded fountain. Between innings, the water spouts high into the air, an effect that is even more spectacular at night, when the falls are backlit by a multicolored display. There is nothing else quite like it in baseball.

The installation of grass here finally gave renowned groundskeeper George Toma a field worthy of his skill. The surface is among the lushest in baseball, a far cry from the artificial turf with dirt cutouts for bases of a few years ago. With

TODD JONES "Kauffman Stadium is actually one of my favorite ballparks in the country because it's maybe thirty to thirty-five years old and it's built just like these brand-new ones are today. It makes me wonder about the marvel that it had to have been, with the restaurant out in left field, thirty years ago. It had to be unprecedented. And the fact that once they changed it from turf to grass, just how beautiful the playing surface is. There's never a bad hop there. I go running prior to the game up on the concourses of all the ballparks. Outside of Dodger Stadium, it is the cleanest concourse I've ever seen. It's a great place. It's a beautiful ballpark, way ahead of its time."

FRANK TANANA "One of the prettiest ballparks I ever played in—I remember it was my first game in the big leagues—was Royals Stadium. Royals Stadium was a gorgeous stadium with the fountains and even the turf, which I'm not a big fan of, but it was a gorgeous place, and I remember losing my first ball game there. But still, it was quite a thrill to walk out there, with probably about 110 degrees off that turf, early-September day. The other amazing thing about that ballpark: I never won there. Nineteen, twenty years of pitching in the American League, and I never won a game in Royals Stadium."

GLENDON RUSCH "It's one of the most beautiful baseball stadiums to play in any league. It's got the waterfalls in center field, the best groundskeeper in baseball, I think, George Toma. It's a great pitcher's park, a good mound, too."

◆ *Home of the Kansas City Royals*

◆ *Kansas City, Missouri: Interstate 70, Interstate 435, and Blue Ridge Cutoff*

◆ *Built 1973*

◆ *Opening Day: April 10, 1973*

◆ *Cost: $70 Million*

◆ *Seating Capacity: 40,625*

◆ *Largest Crowd: 42,633 (October 9, 1980)*

◆ *Formal Name: Ewing M. Kauffman Stadium*

◆ *Former Name: Royals Stadium, 1973–1995*

DIMENSIONS	LF	LCF	CF	RCF	RF
(1973)	330	375	405	375	330
(1992)	330	385	410	385	330
(1999)	330	375	410	375	330

a capacity that has remained at 40,625 since the ballpark opened, Kauffman is among the smallest parks in baseball. As a result, the seating is superb, and only the farthest rows in the upper deck offer distant views.

Unfortunately, Kansas City is a small-market city, and the resultant lack of revenue has prevented the Royals from fielding a contender since the glory days of the eighties. Sellouts are rare, and it remains to be seen how the changing financial climate of baseball will affect this franchise and its wonderful ballpark.

I was about six, seven years old, and me and my mom would go out . . . watching guys like Frank White, George Brett, John Mayberry, all the guys, Amos Otis. I can remember like it was yesterday.

—KEVIN YOUNG

Kingdome

IF OLYMPIC STADIUM in Montreal is considered the worst stadium in baseball, the Kingdome surely ran a close second. Fortunately, Safeco Field replaced this depressing warehouse in 1999.

Although not located in a cold-weather clime like Montreal or Minnesota, Seattle has its share of inclement, mostly rainy, weather. But given a choice between spending a warm, sunny day outdoors in the beautiful Pacific Northwest or sitting in a dingy gray domed stadium, lots of fans might choose to stay away from the ballpark. It is a credit to the Mariners' organization, which assembled an exciting team that featured Ken Griffey Jr. and Alex Rodriguez, that attendance remained at comparatively high levels during the mid- to late nineties. The fans here were loud and enthusiastic, a great contrast to the dark, dismal surroundings, dominated by concrete, artificial turf, and the charcoal-gray dome.

Major League Baseball has not always been successful in Seattle. A different franchise, the expansion Seattle Pilots, played one dismal season in 1969 at Sicks Stadium, a minor-league ballpark, before moving to Milwaukee in 1970. But Seattle was given another opportunity in 1977 with the expansion Mariners, and although the team has never won a championship, the city has been generally sup-

RUSS DAVIS "The Kingdome to me was like an empty warehouse. It was kind of gloomy, never saw daylight. Good hitter's park. There wasn't a whole lot of character to it. It was kind of outdated. I think it was time for it to go."

portive. Due to the small-market status of Seattle and its less than hospitable ballpark, however, previous Mariners owners tried to move the team to Florida. To cope with the growing disparity in revenues between big-market and small-market franchises, Seattle elected to build a baseball-only field that would persuade the Mariners to remain and, hopefully, stay competitive. It remains to be seen whether the new stadium alone will be enough to increase revenues to a pennant-contending level. In any event, most fans will not miss the Kingdome. Hitters, on the other hand, will miss the cozy dimensions when compared with its successor, the more spacious Safeco Field.

- *Former home of the Seattle Mariners*
- *Seattle, Washington: Fourth Avenue South, South Royal Brougham Way, Occidental Avenue South, and South King Street*
- *Built 1977*
- *Opening Day: April 6, 1977*
- *Final Game: June 27, 1999*
- *Cost: $67 Million*
- *Seating Capacity: 59,059 (1977); 57,748 (1991); 59,084 (1998)*
- *Largest Crowd: 59,579 (October 1, 1997)*
- *Nickname: The Tomb*
- *Former home of NFL's Seattle Seahawks*
- *Replaced in 1999 by Safeco Field*
- *Demolished 2000*

DIMENSIONS	LF	LCF	CF	RCF	RF
(1977)	315	375	405	375	315
(1991)	331	376	405	352	314

JASON SCHMIDT "Kingdome—I was in awe, 'cause I was sitting in the outfield looking down on the players. It was exciting, you know? I was looking down and seeing the players, even if they were not good players back then, they were guys that I have in my mind still."

RICHIE SEXSON "It was hard for me to fathom playing in something like that [the Kingdome], because it was so big. You just dream of getting there and playing and things like that. You . . . want to believe that you're going to get there, but it's mostly just a dream when you're that young. I was about eight or ten, somewhere around there, first time I saw it."

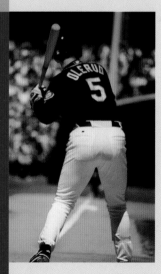

JOHN OLERUD "First big-league ballpark I ever remember seeing is the Kingdome in Seattle. And that was a big deal at the time, and just exciting being there for a big-league ball game."

Arena baseball at its finest. There's a lot of hitters in baseball that are going to be sad to see that one go.

—TODD ZEILE

RICK MONDAY "My first time was actually the L.A. Coliseum after the Dodgers had moved out to Los Angeles. I grew up in the L.A. area, and my first trip to the ballpark was wearing a Little League uniform. It was Little League Day on a Sunday afternoon with thousands of others seated way down the right-field line and watching people that had a major-league uniform on. I thought they were basically gods. I mean, here it is in the Coliseum."

DARRYL BROCK (AUTHOR) "When the Dodgers arrived they played at the Coliseum, which seemed to combine qualities of the two old local parks [Wrigley Field and Gilmore Field] and form a strikingly mixed message: the classic peristyle structure, with its echoes of the '32 Olympics, together with the huge circus-like net that formed the left-field barrier. A strange baseball setting, at once ponderous and transient."

Los Angeles Memorial Coliseum

THIS STADIUM WAS BUILT to host the 1932 Olympic Games. It was adapted for the Dodgers while they waited for the ballpark in Chavez Ravine to be built. Due to the physical limitations of this structure, the ultrashort foul-line dimensions here were absurd for the major leagues. For example, the Dodgers had a first baseman and outfielder named Wally Moon, a left-handed hitter who had a knack for hitting baseballs to the opposite field, known now as inside-outing the ball. Moon's rather diminutive home runs were called Moon Shots. On the other hand, the 42-foot fence above the left-field wall turned what would have been home runs at Ebbets Field into singles or doubles. And Dodger great Duke Snider's home run total went from forty to fifteen when the team moved here.

One number that did increase was the attendance. The Dodgers drew close to two million fans in 1958, almost doubling their final season at Ebbets, confirming owner Walter O'Malley's belief in the potential popularity of Major League Baseball on the West Coast.

BOB APODACA "My first recollection of a Major League Baseball park, growing up as a child, was the L.A. Coliseum. My father took me there when—I don't know, I was probably eight or nine—and my first impression was seeing the Chinese Wall, they used to call it, in left field, it was like 250 feet down the left-field line with approximately a forty-foot- or fifty-foot-high netting. And I remember Wally Moon hitting several home runs to the opposite field—he was a left-handed hitter—and they used to call them Moon Shots. I remember Frank Howard, who was a young Frank Howard playing left field, hitting prodigious home runs over the fence. I remember Tommy Davis hitting line drives off the fence. And then a young Sandy Koufax, Drysdale—those were very, very memorable moments for me."

AL HRABOSKY "I was probably eleven years old . . . That's where the Dodgers were playing before Chavez Ravine was built, and I was out in right field, and Duke Snider hit a home run and I jumped up like everyone else in the crowd and I threw up my Dodger Dog!"

MARCEL LACHEMANN "First [stadium] I ever saw was the Coliseum. That's because I was born and raised out here. We never had Major League Baseball until the Dodgers came out here in the Coliseum. And of course it was a football stadium that I'd gone to as a kid a lot, to see football, so it was a little unusual to see that transformed into a baseball field. Ninety thousand people in there a lot of times, too, so it was kind of neat. I was seventeen. I saw those Moon Shots, and I saw the Dodgers when they came out here from Brooklyn. They were nothing; they lost that first year. And the next year, they won the whole thing."

- ◆ *Former home of the Los Angeles Dodgers*
- ◆ *Los Angeles, California: Santa Barbara Avenue, Hoover Avenue, Exposition Boulevard, and Figueroa Street*
- ◆ *Built 1923*
- ◆ *Opening Day: April 18, 1958*
- ◆ *Final Game: September 20, 1961*
- ◆ *Seating Capacity: 74,000 (1923); 105,000 (1932, for Olympics); 93,000 (1958)*
- ◆ *Largest Crowd: 92,706 (October 6, 1959)*
- ◆ *Also known as the L.A. Coliseum*
- ◆ *Former home of NFL's Los Angeles Rams*
- ◆ *Former home of NFL's Los Angeles Raiders*

DIMENSIONS	LF	LCF	CF	RCF	RF
(1958)	251	320	425	440	301
(1961)	251	320	420	380	300

McAfee

T HE ATHLETICS HAD MOVED from Kansas City in 1968, where they were known both for losing games and for supplying the Yankees with a steady stream of talented players in exchange for mostly cash while owner Charlie Finley tried to keep his franchise afloat. Before Oakland, the A's hadn't stayed long in Kansas City, having only moved there from Philadelphia in 1955. But with the advent of the free-agent draft in 1965, teams no longer had to compete with one another to sign top high school and college players. The athletes were simply chosen by the teams in inverse order of their previous year's standings. With the A's finishing at the bottom of the American

League so often, they were able to draft players like Reggie Jackson, Vida Blue, and Jim "Catfish" Hunter. And so by 1972 the A's were a powerhouse, winning three straight World Championships. The players, though, soon demanded more money than Finley was willing to pay, and the team was broken up. Unable to compete, the A's began drawing crowds on some occasions of fewer than 1,000 fans—hence the term Oakland Mausoleum. Finley finally sold the team in 1980.

The new owners, the Levi-Strauss family, worked hard to bring the fans back, spending money both on better ballplayers and on ballpark renovation.

RICKEY HENDERSON "My first time in person, I went to the ballpark and I really saw Reggie Jackson play. I think Reggie Jackson hit a home run, and that excited me. And I think that drew my attention."

MARK LANGSTON "I remember going to the Oakland Coliseum as a kid and I was totally awestruck. Baltimore Orioles were my favorite team, so just to go there and see that was pretty incredible."

- ◆ *Home of the Oakland Athletics*
- ◆ *Oakland, California: Nimitz Freeway, Hegenberger Road, 66th Avenue, and San Leandro Boulevard*
- ◆ *Built 1968*
- ◆ *Opening Day: April 17, 1968*
- ◆ *Cost: $25.5 Million*
- ◆ *Renovation Cost (1996): $200 Million*
- ◆ *Seating Capacity: 50,219 (1968); 47,450 (1991); 45,177 (1998); 43,012 (2000)*
- ◆ *Largest Crowd: 50,792 (September 1, 1997)*
- ◆ *Formerly known as Oakland Coliseum, 1968–1999; Network Associates Coliseum, 1999-2004*
- ◆ *Nickname: The Oakland Mausoleum (1970s only)*
- ◆ *Home of NFL's Oakland Raiders*

DIMENSIONS	LF	LCF	CF	RCF	RF
(1968)	330	378	410	378	330
(1992)	330	375	400	375	330

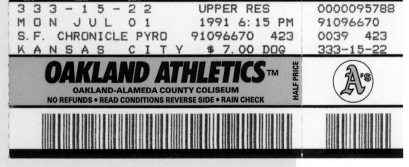

By 1991 the only problem with the stadium was the large expanse of foul territory between the baselines and the stands. One could not sit quite as close to the action in the lower deck as in some other parks. However, the immaculately kept field—the lush grass, called Prescription Athletic Turf, is mowed in crosscut fashion, creating a checkerboard effect—the spotless stands, and the scenic, tree-filled view beyond center field more than made up for this single shortcoming. There was scarcely a more enjoyable place to watch a ball game.

Before the 1998 construction of the huge addition to benefit Al Davis's Oakland Raiders of the NFL, this ballpark might have been the most underrated in all of baseball. Unfortunately, thousands of seats and numerous luxury boxes were constructed beyond center field, eliminating the view. This monolith of an addition stands empty during A's games, turning what was a pastoral setting into a charmless one. The A's also alienated fans by changing the name of the stadium in 1999. Perhaps the A's will find another home—a baseball-only field in Sacramento or San Jose—and leave the Coliseum to the Raiders.

ANDY FOX "The first time I ever walked into a big-league stadium was the Oakland Coliseum. My dad took me to a ball game, and the only thing I remember was my father pointing out, watching the left fielder get a whole bunch of fly balls, and it happened to be Brian Downing of the California Angels. He was showing how he was working the wall, how to play the wall."

OMAR VIZQUEL "The first time I saw a major-league ballpark was in Oakland. It was my Opening Day—April 3, 1989—and I was pretty impressed."

Memorial Stadium

BALTIMORE'S MEMORIAL STADIUM, built in 1950, is a solid brick building situated in an odd, not-quite-urban, not-quite-suburban neighborhood. It is still standing at this writing, though it is no longer used by the Orioles or the NFL's Baltimore franchise, and is scheduled for demolition. The wonderful Camden Yards was built to replace Memorial, so baseball fans do not especially miss this stadium. Although baseball traditionalists usually protest the destruction of any stadium, when Memorial is inevitably razed protests will probably be minimal.

Memorial was difficult to get to, either by car or by mass transit, and the parking lots featured bumper-to-bumper parking: acres and acres of cars crammed together mere inches apart. Once parked, you could leave the premises only if the car directly in front of or behind you moved first.

Inside the park was a bigger problem: It simply wasn't a good place to watch a game. In big-league ballparks, not everyone can sit close to the action;

in fact, a lot of fans sit closer to the parking lot than to home plate. But in Memorial, even a seat in a ground-level section close to the playing field did not ensure a quality view. Thousands of seats were situated under the overhang from the deck above, twenty or thirty rows deep, foul line to foul line. Lost on those spectators was the opportunity to watch the arc of a pop-up or a

JOHN SCHUERHOLZ (BRAVES GM) "What I recall the most vividly about my first trip to a major-league ballpark, which happened to be Baltimore's Memorial Stadium, my hometown of Baltimore, was how excited I was. My dad was a minor-league baseball player and we talked about baseball, and baseball was a big part of our household at the time. And when I was old enough to go to a game and have some real enjoyment and be able to understand what was going on, my father took me. And what I remember most is how as a young boy, everything seemed so large, the people I met who were his friends seemed large, their handshakes seemed to envelop me when I shook their hands. My father said, 'Be sure to shake their hands firmly, son. Don't give them a dead fish.' And I'm meeting all of these guys he played baseball with and basketball with in Baltimore. And then, as we walked up the tunnel, the walkway, and I saw this field, it looked like the most beautiful thing in the world."

DENNY NEAGLE "I grew up in the Baltimore area so the first stadium I ever saw was Memorial Stadium. . . . I grew up learning to be a baseball historian—purist, my dad kind of instilled that in me. I still feel that way today, and I'll always remember going to that park and watching Jim Palmer and Scotty McGregor, and obviously the great rivalry they had with the Yankees, too. . . . I think my first game, I was probably about seven years old. I used to sit there and say to him—probably not until I was about fourteen, fifteen years old, that I started saying—'You know what, Dad, I think I might have a chance to do this . . . You watch, Dad, one of these days you're going to watch me pitch in one of these parks.'"

I'm from Baltimore. In high school we had our all-star game at Memorial Stadium, and that was the first time coming out of the locker room. You know, just seeing all the fans out there, and all the seats in the stands—I mean, that blew me away.

— BRIAN JORDAN

deep fly ball, to observe the angle the fielders take to intercept the ball's path, to marvel at the majestic parabola of a long blast. They might as well have been watching it on television, which many of them did on monitors suspended from the bottom of the very deck that was obscuring their view. And even in the seats that were not obstructed by the overhang, there seemed to be an odd configuration about the place: In both the lower and upper deck, it felt as though the pitcher's mound should have been placed somewhere near third base.

Fans could not have been more enthusiastic about the coming of Camden Yards. No one lamented the loss of Memorial. And when Camden Yards opened in the revitalized downtown Inner Harbor, the fans were proven right.

- *Former home of the Baltimore Orioles*
- *Baltimore, Maryland: East 33rd Street (Babe Ruth Plaza), 36th Street, Ellerslie Avenue, and Ednor Road*
- *Built 1950*
- *Opening Day: April 15, 1954*
- *Final Game: September 30, 1991*
- *Cost: $6.5 Million*
- *Seating Capacity: 31,000 (1950); 53,371 (1991)*
- *Largest Crowd: 54,458 (October 9, 1966)*
- *Home of the International League Baltimore Orioles, 1950–1953*
- *Former home of NFL's Baltimore Colts*
- *Replaced in 1992 by Camden Yards*

DIMENSIONS	LF	LCF	CF	RCF	RF
(1954)	309	446	445	446	309
(1991)	309	390	410	390	309

CAL RIPKEN JR.
"I think the first time you walk out to a big-league field, no matter where you are, that signifies the most special stadium to you. Memorial Stadium was my field, it was the home ballpark for the Orioles, and I came on as a pinch runner . . . It was the first time that I actually felt that a baseball field was like a stage. You went out, there were really bright lights and it was all filled, and I had never been in a situation like that. I had been to the stadium before, I had worked out early in the day before the people started to fill in. But it was such a different feeling once the game had started and once it had filled with people."

WADE BOGGS "Old Memorial Stadium, I walked in and was in awe. I mean, I had finally made it to the big leagues and here I am in the same place that I was watching the . . . World Series. I grew up in Tampa, Florida, so I'd never been to a big-league stadium as a kid. We just had Al Lopez [Field], where the Reds trained, and that was basically all I had ever gone to."

ANDY MACPHAIL (CUBS PRESIDENT)
"Baltimore's Memorial Stadium in the late fifties. There was something exciting about moving from the dark concourse . . . into the bright sunlight and the green grass. I would sit behind the plate with my older brother with seventy-five cents in my pocket waiting for the top of the fifth to get ice cream and a Coke."

Metrodome

THE MINNESOTA TWINS began playing in the American League in 1961, having moved from Washington, D.C., where they were called the Senators: "First in war, first in peace, last in the American League." The newly relocated and renamed team was not much more successful, until they captured the pennant in 1965.

The Twins played at Metropolitan Stadium in nearby Bloomington until 1982. The Met was known to be a decent baseball park, similar to County Stadium in Milwaukee. But it was replaced by the Metrodome, which was among the last of the multipurpose stadiums to be built. Now, less than twenty years later, the Twins have announced that the stadium is obsolete and that baseball is doomed in Minnesota without a new ballpark. And so it goes.

The most notable aspects of the Metrodome are the Baggie—the blue plastic material that covers the right-field wall—and the incredible noise level attained when the stadium is full and the fans are screaming.

The problem with a nonretractable domed stadium in Minneapolis is, ironically, the weather. It's frigid here for much of the year, so when the temperature finally rises above freezing, people don't want to spend their time indoors watching baseball. On gorgeous Sundays, fans gather slowly, lingering in the warm sunlight before entering the gloom of the Dome. In most other cities, fans seem eager to enter the ballpark, to be entertained. Not so in the Twin Cities. Although the Metrodome is smaller and not as monolithic as other domes, with its translucent cloth-covered roof, it is still an unlikely place to spend an all-too-rare beautiful day in the Land of a Thousand Lakes.

We played the playoffs in 1987 with Detroit and Minnesota.

I couldn't see [the ball] there. Matter of fact, it reminded me so

much of the Astrodome. Everybody was close up on you, the

fans were just deafening. I couldn't hear myself think.

—BILL MADLOCK

- *Home of the Minnesota Twins*
- *Minneapolis, Minnesota: Eleventh Avenue South, Fifth Street South, Chicago Avenue South, and Fourth Street South*
- *Built 1982*
- *Opening Day: April 6, 1982*
- *Cost: $62 Million*
- *Seating Capacity: 54,711 (1982); 55,883 (1989); 48,678 (1998)*
- *Largest Crowd: 55,376 (October 25, 1987)*
- *Formal Name: Hubert H. Humphrey Metrodome*
- *Nickname: The Homerdome*
- *Home of NFL's Minnesota Vikings*
- *Measured loudest ballpark in major leagues (118 decibels during 1987 World Series)*

DIMENSIONS	LF	LCF	CF	RCF	RF
(1991)	343	385	408	367	327

TONY CLARK "I remember the first year I came up. Everybody had talked about how they could lose a fly ball in the roof. The very first BP I had in the ballpark, the ball went up, I went running after it, and I realized very early on how quickly you can lose the ball in the roof, and how silly you can look when it bounces a hundred feet from you."

DAVE BERGMAN "The Metrodome when fully seated is probably one of the loudest places you've ever been in your life. It's also kind of an unusual stadium, especially when you're playing the outfield. They've got these orange lights at the top of the stadium, and when a ball goes up, not only do you lose it in the roof, but you have a tough time getting it out of those orange lights."

MIKE KRUKOW "We came out of spring training in 1982 with the Phillies, and we were going to go up to Minnesota for a two-game exhibition prior to the season starting. It was a brand-new field, so we were all excited to get up there. We leave Clearwater where the Phillies trained and we get up there in Minnesota, we were freezing our ass off. We go to this place and we couldn't believe how cheap the turf was; it was terrible. They had this big Baggie over the fence. I'm thinking: This is a brand-new place? This thing is a dog. Anyway, I was the first guy to pitch there. I didn't know anybody on the Twins team. They had a bunch of kids coming up, and they just kicked my ass. Kent Hrbek hit the longest home run; he hit it about eight hundred feet. It was a cold place; they had the fans going. And you couldn't hear. The acoustics were terrible. You'd yell to your second baseman, it felt like you were playing in a vacuum. The good fans of Minnesota—they are great fans up there; I don't know how they've put up with that place for as long as they have. I think they'd rather have the park they had before the Metrodome."

Metropolitan Stadium

JESSE VENTURA (MINNESOTA GOVERNOR)
"I rode my bike to . . . Metropolitan in Minneapolis. I remember Jim Gentile hit two grand slam home runs. I was eleven or twelve, something like that."

ROY WHITE "Metropolitan Stadium in Minnesota —very cheery atmosphere to play in, the fans were close to you, great hitting background, they had a nice black backdrop in center field and so you saw the ball well there at home plate. And I remember just the day games there, there was always a sunny, bright, beautiful day; and there were nice fans out in Minnesota; and they always had those good teams with Harmon Killebrew and Carew and Tony Oliva. And a good PA announcer with a very unique voice . . . They had a big scoreboard up in right-center field, and I remember going in there and them talking about the ball that Reggie Jackson hit off the top of that scoreboard. It was one of the famous long balls of that time in the seventies."

RON SCHUELER "A great old ballpark, good hitter's park. You could see it; the ball jumped pretty well there. . . . Baseball should be outdoors, and I think they lost something when they moved inside."

BILLY SAMPLE "Outside of the fact that they would occasionally play these 10:00 A.M. games when the Golden Gophers [the University of Minnesota's football team] also had a game on a Saturday, I remember in the outfield at the Met they had mosquitoes that would eat insect repellent as an appetizer. You'd look down at your sanitary socks, and you were swatting them the whole time, there'd be splotches of red on the front and back of your sanitaries. It got a little cold, too, early and late in the season. Leon Roberts and I once went sleeveless in about forty degrees with the wind-chill factor of about ten. And of course the macho thing to do is, once you start sleeveless, you *cannot* come back into the dugout and put sleeves on. So when the temperature drops to about *minus* ten, you've just got to suffer, hope you got a couple of hits to go along with the pain."

RARELY IS AN OLD BELOVED BALLPARK replaced with a new stadium that is held in equal or greater esteem. The only example that comes to mind is in Detroit, where the much-appreciated Comerica Park succeeded venerable Tiger Stadium. In Minnesota, the Metrodome, in use for only about twenty years, is widely disliked, while the old Met is remembered quite fondly. (And it is still mentioned frequently as the site of what is now the Mall of America, the Met having been demolished in 1985 to make way for the mall.) The city feared losing the NFL's Vikings—the winter weather in Minnesota is not conducive to playing football outdoors—so they built the domed multipurpose Metrodome.

In the sixties, the Twins were known as a heavy-hitting, slow-footed team. So the groundskeepers would tailor the field, sloping the baselines so that weak grounders would roll foul. Before the 1965 World Series, in which the Twins met the speedy Los Angeles Dodgers, sand was mixed with the infield dirt to try to slow down the base runners. Umpires forced the grounds crew to remove much of the sand.

The Met had a grassy knoll outside the left-field fence. A batter once belted a home run into this area, and the ball struck someone in the head—shocking proof that you could get hurt watching a Major League Baseball game. There are no longer any grassy picnic areas in the big leagues.

DIMENSIONS	LF	LCF	CF	RCF	RF
(1961)	329	365	412	365	329
(1977)	343	360	402	370	330

- *Former home of the Minnesota Twins*
- *Bloomington, Minnesota: Cedar Avenue, 24th Avenue, and Killebrew Drive*
- *Built 1956*
- *Opening Day: April 21, 1961*
- *Final Game: September 30, 1981*
- *Seating Capacity: 18,200 (1956); 45,919 (1961)*
- *Largest Crowd: 50,596 (October 14, 1965)*
- *Nickname: The Met*
- *Former home of the American Association Minneapolis Millers, 1956–1960*
- *Former home of NFL's Minnesota Vikings*
- *Replaced by Hubert H. Humphrey Metrodome, 1982*

MIKE CUBBAGE "[Metropolitan] was where I played most of my big-league career with the Twins. Starting the year there in April with snow piled up twelve to fourteen feet high in the parking lot. Occasionally we'd get a lucky spring day where it's about 55 degrees. The machine they had to bring the tarp out was automated. It came from under the fence in right field. The thing would come out the first time fine, but if it had to come out two or three times for a rain delay, the tarp was so heavy, they really struggled getting it back on the field."

Mile High Stadium

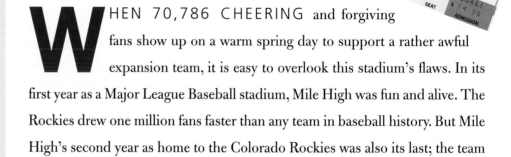

LANCE PARRISH "I had the opportunity to play in Mile High Stadium both in the minor leagues and the major leagues. I played there when I was with the Evansville Triplets, which was the Triple A team for Detroit, and I played there with the Pirates later on in my career. The great thing about it was . . . the ball always traveled well. When I was in the minors, a guy who's a hitting coach by the name of Rick Renick almost hit the horse statue that stands above the right-field bleachers, the big white bronco that they have up there. When we saw him do that in BP, I think everybody was just amazed at how far the ball went. I think that word got around that all you really wanted to try and do was to get the ball in the air there. And I think more guys screwed up their swings at Mile High Stadium trying to get the ball in the air."

DARRYL HAMILTON "A Ping-Pong game or a pinball game in a baseball atmosphere. Anything could happen at that ballpark. It's not uncommon to have the Denver Broncos' scores going up on the board. Fifteen, sixteen runs is very common in that park."

GENE CLINES "One thing about Mile High: No lead's ever a safe lead in that ballpark. You could be up by five runs and it feels like a tie ball game, because the ball flies out of there so well."

WHEN 70,786 CHEERING and forgiving fans show up on a warm spring day to support a rather awful expansion team, it is easy to overlook this stadium's flaws. In its first year as a Major League Baseball stadium, Mile High was fun and alive. The Rockies drew one million fans faster than any team in baseball history. But Mile High's second year as home to the Colorado Rockies was also its last; the team moved to brand-new Coors Field for the 1995 season.

Mile High was not built as a multipurpose stadium. It started as a baseball park, built for the minor-league Denver Bears in 1948. Over the years, decks were added, stacked one on top of the other, with an entire separate structure added in left field, increasing the seating capacity of the stadium from its original 10,000 to well over 76,000. This separate structure, which for baseball configuration extended from the left-field foul line all the way to center field, actually floats on water and is movable, which created goal-line-to-goal-line seating for the NFL's Denver Broncos football games.

The stadium was named for the altitude in Denver: 5,280 or so feet above sea level. The upper deck here, then, could be called Mile-and-a-Half High, and it is an aerobic workout away from being able to watch a baseball game at a comfortable distance. Aside from the poor baseball sight lines, this place was actually a lot of fun because of the fans. A particularly entertaining fan activity was Rocky Mountain Thunder, which took full advantage of the stadium's structure. The two additional decks atop the original structure are made of steel, not concrete. So when

Mile High, Denver:

unbelievable. First

time I was called up,

seventy thousand.

I was kind of nervous,

to be honest.

—RONDELL WHITE

fans wanted to incite a rally or merely make a lot of noise, they stamped their feet. When thousands of people stomp fast and hard, the result is an exceedingly loud roar that does indeed sound like thunder. There was also the rhythmic chanting: One side of the stadium would yell, "Go!"; the other side would reply, "Rockies!" Great fun. Despite errors, missed relay throws, and other assorted mishaps, fans remained unfazed.

The Rockies no longer play at Mile High. While Coors Field is a much finer baseball facility, it does seem as if some of the innocent fun of that first-year expansion team is gone.

DIMENSIONS	LF	LCF	CF	RCF	RF
(1993)	333	366	423	400	370

- *Former home of the Colorado Rockies*
- *Denver, Colorado: Eliot Street, 20th Avenue, Clay Street, and 17th Avenue*
- *Built 1948*
- *Opening Day: April 9, 1993 (National League)*
- *Final Game: August 11, 1994*
- *Seating Capacity: 10,000 (1948); 76,037 (1992)*
- *Largest Crowd: 80,227 (April 9, 1993)*
- *Former Name: Bears Stadium, 1948–1968*
- *Former home of NFL's Denver Broncos*
- *Former home of the Triple A Denver Bears and Denver Zephyrs*
- *Replaced by Coors Field, 1995*

Minute Maid Park

WHEN A BASEBALL FRANCHISE moves from an old stadium to a new facility, comparisons are inevitable. While fans are concerned with comfort and sight lines, the players discuss playability. Some ballparks are known as hitters' parks: The outfield fences are close, the wind often blows out, or the air is thin so the ball flies. Other stadiums are known as pitchers' parks: The ball doesn't leave the yard very often, the outfield is where fly balls go to die.

Perhaps the greatest change for a ball club in recent memory was the Houston Astros' move from the spacious Astrodome to the cozy confines of Minute Maid Park (formerly called Enron Field), where home runs are struck often and far. Like most stadiums built since Camden Yards in Baltimore

opened in 1992, Minute Maid Park has a number of nostalgic features and quirks. Most obvious is the incline in deep center field, a sort of grassy knoll built up beyond the traditional warning track and extending to the wall. This feature was modeled after the incline as Crosley Field in Cincinnati,

but with a big difference: At Crosley the incline began near the point where the left fielder would normally position himself, and so it was a constant factor for the outfielders. But the incline at Minute Maid Park, 420 feet from home plate, won't figure into play very often.

Although Minute Maid Park is located in downtown Houston, not much skyline is visible. One structure that is prominent, just beyond the left-

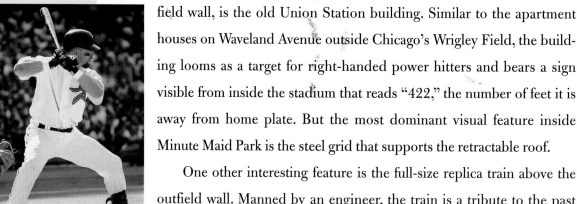

JEFF BAGWELL "It's a beautiful ballpark. Fans have come out. It's baseball outside, which has not been here since—what, '65, I think. It's an exciting place; it's a pleasure to play here."

BILL SPIERS "What's neat about [Enron] is, it's a retractable-roof stadium, but it looks like an outdoor stadium when the roof is open. It's not your typical dome that you can't open. It's American League baseball; it's played here now instead of National League. It's a hitter's park, and big numbers are going on the scoreboard, and long games are happening here."

BILLY WILLIAMS "If you look down to left field here at Enron, you see [a reminder of] the Fenway Park wall. The ball hits the wall and the shortstop has to be involved in it because the ball bounces back to the shortstop."

JOHN STERLING (BROADCASTER) "Enron Field is unbelievably exciting. And it's being knocked among some people in baseball, old fuddy-duddies, because the left-field wall is very short, which it is, but . . . center field is long, right field is more than adequate. They have a train that runs on top of the wall, it's high-tech, state-of-the-art, it's right downtown, it's fabulous."

DAN GLADDEN "I think Enron Field has a lot of old ballparks in it. Straightaway center field has a little bit of a hill with the flagpole still in play. It has the scoreboard in left field that comes out about thirty feet. There are a lot of nooks and crannies. I think for the Houston area, it's something that the ball club and the city needed."

field wall, is the old Union Station building. Similar to the apartment houses on Waveland Avenue outside Chicago's Wrigley Field, the building looms as a target for right-handed power hitters and bears a sign visible from inside the stadium that reads "422," the number of feet it is away from home plate. But the most dominant visual feature inside Minute Maid Park is the steel grid that supports the retractable roof.

One other interesting feature is the full-size replica train above the outfield wall. Manned by an engineer, the train is a tribute to the past glory of Union Station. It sits atop a bridgelike limestone structure; when an Astros player hits a home run, the engineer blows the whistle and runs the train along the track from center to left field. This is certainly a step beyond the scoreboard cartoon train in Pittsburgh's Three Rivers Stadium.

The railroad bridge is built above the shortest left-field distance in the National League. While baseball stadiums used to be designed to suit the team that was to play there, this ballpark is hitter-friendly as well as fan-friendly, and the Astros are faced with a difficult adjustment after their thirty-five-year stint in the Astrodome.

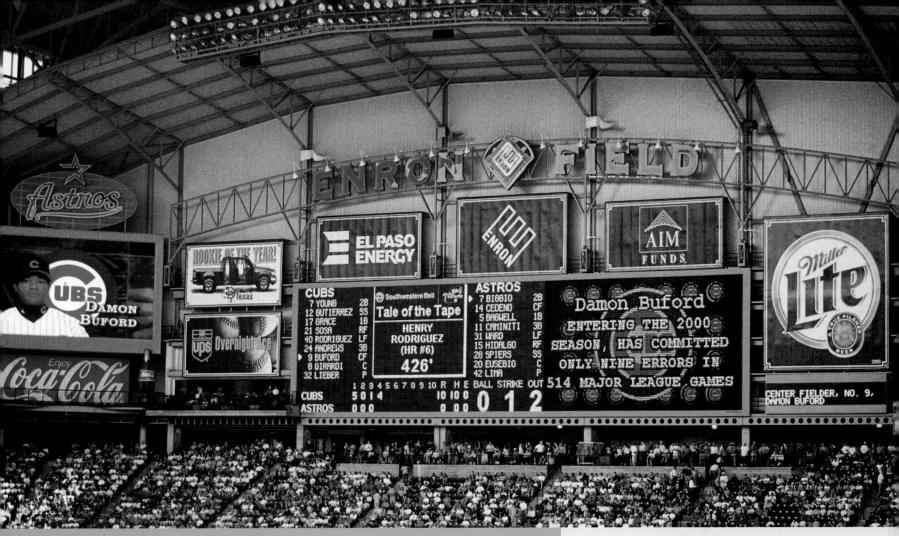

- ◆ *Home of the Houston Astros*

- ◆ *Houston, Texas: Crawford Street, Texas Street, Congress Street, and Highway 59*

- ◆ *Built 2000*

- ◆ *Opening Day: April 7, 2000*

- ◆ *Cost: $248 Million*

- ◆ *Seating Capacity: 40,950*

- ◆ *Largest Crowd: 43,189 (September 2, 2000)*

- ◆ *Replaced Astrodome, 2000*

DIMENSIONS	LF	LCF	CF	RCF	RF
(2000)	315	362	436	373	326

Municipal
Stadium
(Cleveland)

BEFORE THIS STADIUM was torn down in 1997, its most distinctive feature was outside the ballpark: the huge Wahoo Indians logo that towered above the entrance as you approached from Lake Shore Boulevard. This grinning Indian, Chief Wahoo, has been a symbol of the Cleveland Indians for many generations of baseball fans, and remains one of the most recognizable, long-lived logos in professional sports. It proudly welcomed fans to an otherwise inhospitable facility.

Municipal Stadium was often referred to as the Mistake by the Lake. This stadium was built to attract the 1932 Summer Olympics, which instead ended up in Los Angeles. In order to justify its construction, the city of Cleveland persuaded the Indians, who were playing in League Park at the time, to play some weekend games at Municipal. The city did not maintain League Park properly, so as it deteriorated, the Indians had no choice but to play all their games in Municipal. Its location, close to Lake Erie, made for less than pleasant conditions when the wind blew in from the water. Its size, with a seating capacity of

DAVE NEMEC (AUTHOR) "It was both the best and the worst place to watch a ball game. When the Indians were a great team in the 1950s and late 1940s and they drew crowds of upwards of seventy thousand, there was no more wonderful place ever to watch a ball game. The place was really hopping. It was a huge, cavernous stadium. When the team started falling on hard times in the late 1950s through almost the mid-1990s, it was absolutely the worst place to watch a ball game. You'd get five or six thousand people there in a stadium that could seat over eighty thousand. There was very little crowd noise, as the Indians were usually losing. You felt lonely, isolated, and quite depressed."

BOB MURPHY (BROADCASTER) "What I remember is the tremendous size of the place and how terribly cold that building would get. It would get into July before it would really start to warm up. It was a massive building, not good for baseball at all."

BRIAN ANDERSON "First stadium as a kid was old Cleveland Stadium. We all had our own personal vendor. And we banged on the seats, maybe we could get a rally, which was two or three times a year."

CARLOS BAERGA "I never thought that it would be so impressive. I used to see ballparks in Puerto Rico, but not something like that, to see so many fans coming to the game."

◆ *Former home of the Cleveland Indians*

◆ *Cleveland, Ohio: West 3rd Street, Boudreau Boulevard, and Lake Shore Boulevard*

◆ *Built 1931*

◆ *Opening Day: July 31, 1932*

◆ *Final Game: October 3, 1993*

◆ *Cost: $3 Million*

◆ *Seating Capacity: 78,000 (1930); 74,483 (1991)*

◆ *Largest Crowd: 86,563 (September 12, 1954)*

◆ *Also known as Cleveland Stadium*

◆ *Nickname: The Mistake by the Lake*

◆ *Former home of NFL's Cleveland Browns*

◆ *Replaced by Jacobs Field, 1994*

◆ *Demolished 1996*

DIMENSIONS	LF	LCF	CF	RCF	RF
(1931)	322	435	470	435	322
(1991)	328	400	415	400	328

78,000, resulted in the large majority of games having more empty seats than fans. It was always clear that Municipal was simply not built for baseball.

Fortunately for Cleveland fans, Jacobs Field replaced Municipal in 1994 and is perennially sold out. The Indians have been contenders ever since the new stadium opened. Sometimes a new ballpark makes all the difference.

GREG VAUGHN "Wow . . . Cleveland, old Cleveland Stadium. I was twenty-one years old, so it was an experience . . . Even when I watched it on TV, I said, 'I'm going to be down there someday.'"

DAVID CONE "It was in Kansas City; it was the old Municipal ballpark. My father took me when I was a young child, and the first thing I remember was how green the grass was. 'Cause George Toma was a great groundskeeper and had the most beautiful field in the big leagues. I'll never forget the look of the green field. I think I was six or seven years old."

DAVE MAGADAN "I was maybe six years old, seven years old. What I do remember about Municipal was that my father saved the life of a lady. We were sitting over the third-base dugout, and somebody hit a line drive into the stands, and she wasn't looking, she was talking to somebody . . . and the ball was coming right at her temple and my father stuck his hand out and blocked it. That's what I remember."

JOE SIMPSON "First major-league park I went into was old Municipal Stadium in Kansas City, and it was for a doubleheader. It was my first year of college, actually, and the Royals were a year or so old. They were a new team in baseball, but they started in the old ballpark . . . What was beautiful was the greenness of the field. George Toma, the famous groundskeeper for the Kansas City sports teams, was the groundskeeper then. Between games of the doubleheader, I was so impressed by the fact the groundskeepers all lined up about arm's-length apart on the foul line down the right-field line and all had a bucket in their hand. They walked, arm's-length apart, all the way across the outfield to the left-field foul line and picked any blade of grass that was out of place, that had been kicked up in game one, any piece of trash that had blown on the field. Any little mar on that green grass was taken care of by those guys, as they looked like ants marching across the field."

GARY PETERS "I won my first game as a major-league player in the old stadium in Kansas City, hit a home run and pitched seven innings for the win."

Municipal Stadium (Kansas City)

BEFORE ATHLETICS OWNER Charles O. Finley moved this franchise to Oakland in 1968, the Kansas City Athletics played in this old ballpark. The Athletics were always an also-ran to the perennial pennant-winning Yankees, but in 1965 Finley decided to try to emulate the success of the Yankees. Yankee Stadium was built in 1923 and was configured to suit slugger Babe Ruth, a left-handed hitter. The Yankees' right-field fence thus stood only 296 feet from home plate, one of the major league's shortest distances. Through the years, the Yanks would field a succession of left-handed batters, such as Roger Maris and Joe Pepitone, to take advantage of this short porch. So in Kansas City, Finley built a fence in front of the existing right-field wall at a distance of 296 feet, a Pennant Porch to match that of Yankee Stadium. Baseball Commissioner Ford Frick took a dim view of this and ordered Finley to restore the fence to its previous distance, whereupon the phrase "Half-Pennant Porch" was painted on the fence.

Finley also gained notoriety for maintaining a small zoo beyond the right-field fence. He would occasionally ride one of the inhabitants of the zoo, a mule named Charlie O, around the field before games. If Finley hadn't spent much of the fifties and sixties trading most of his young talent—including Roger Maris—to the Yanks, he might have won more games in Kansas City. Once established in Oakland, though, he won three World Series in the seventies.

DIMENSIONS	LF	LCF	CF	RCF	RF
(1923)	350	408	450	N/A	350
(1955)	312	382	430	382	347
(1969)	369	408	421	382	338

- *Former home of the Kansas City Royals, 1969–1972*
- *Kansas City, Missouri: Twenty-second Street, Brooklyn Avenue, Twenty-first Street, and Euclid Avenue*
- *Built 1923*
- *Opening Day: April 12, 1955 (Kansas City Athletics); April 8, 1969 (Kansas City Royals)*
- *Cost: $400,000*
- *Renovation Cost (1954–1955): $2.5 Million*
- *Seating Capacity: 17,476 (1923); 30,296 (1955); 35,561 (1971)*
- *Largest Crowd: 36,623 (August 3, 1971)*
- *Home of the Negro League Kansas City Monarchs, 1923–1950*
- *Former home of the American League Kansas City Athletics, 1955–1967*

BILL RUSSELL "My first time at a major-league stadium was at Kansas City when the Athletics were there. I was a senior in high school and I went out to watch the Yankees play, and I never in my life could picture a stadium being that big and holding that many people in one park. I was from a small town in Kansas, fifteen thousand people, and you go to a stadium that holds anywhere from forty thousand to fifty thousand people . . . So I was in awe, to go to a game like that, especially to watch the Yankees. Mantle was still playing at that time . . . You never forget that."

Olympic Stadium

THE SECOND MOST frequently asked question of someone who has seen all of the Major League Baseball stadiums is "Which is the worst ballpark?" Though the answer is subjective, a very strong case can be made for Olympic Stadium, or Stade Olympique, which has been a disaster from the outset.

The Big O, built to host the 1976 Olympics, is located in a pleasant area outside downtown Montreal amid a large park and science exposition, easily reachable via the underground Metro. Not much else can be said for it.

The construction cost ran hundreds of millions of dollars over budget, a large portion of which was wasted on a stunningly tall tower erected to control the (supposedly) retractable roof. It worked intermittently before being disman-

tled in 1997. A new roof was installed to replace the hideous orange canopy, by far the worst of any of the domed stadiums.

Like their counterparts in Minnesota, Montreal fans spend a great deal of time indoors during the Canadian winters. They are not likely to waste precious warm summer days and nights sitting in a dark, dingy arena watching a sport that will never be more popular here than hockey. The few fans who do show up are loud, enthusiastic, and supportive. Unfortunately, they have never been rewarded with a championship. The Expos haven't won a pennant since their inception in 1969. With its small-market revenues

and resulting minuscule payroll, the odds for postseason play in Montreal are usually long.

Polls are alleged to have indicated that there is enough fan interest to support a Major League Baseball club here in Quebec's largest city. New Expos ownership is attempting to arrange financing for a baseball-only stadium in downtown Montreal—another struggling franchise looking for a new-ballpark quick fix.

DIMENSIONS	LF	LCF	CF	RCF	RF
(1991)	325	375	404	375	325

Olympic Stadium will always have a place in my heart because that's where I made my major-league debut for the Expos. Actually, [that was] the first time I'd ever been inside of a domed stadium. I grew up with everything being out in the open—St. Louis. I won the game, my first major-league start.

—KIRK RUETER

ANDRES GALARRAGA "I'm kind of scared my first time I see a big-league stadium . . . First one was in Montreal. Olympic Stadium. And I mean, beautiful, exciting, to see the up and down, the cover, and all that stuff."

JERRY MANUEL "Montreal was a nice fun stadium for me because we won ball games there. And at that time it was a packed place. There was a lot of cement around that ballpark, but I enjoyed it. Back in '80, '81, there was a great feeling in that ballpark."

TOM SEAVER "Olympic Stadium was one of the worst stadiums I ever played in, from a fan's standpoint and from the feeling a player has on the field. The service of the field was far less than adequate— it was so bumpy and there were ridges in the outfield. Players sometimes got hurt."

MIKE HAMPTON "It's the worst ballpark I've ever played in in my entire life. It's a horrible place to play—you feel like you're playing in a garage. The fans don't come out to watch the game."

◆ *Home of the Montreal Expos*
◆ *Montreal, Quebec: Rue Sherbrooke, Rue Pius IX, Avenue Pierre-de-Coubertin, and Rue Viau*
◆ *Built 1976*
◆ *Opening Day: April 15, 1977*
◆ *Cost: $770 Million–$1 Billion*
◆ *Seating Capacity: 58,838 (1977); 60,111 (1991); 46,500 (1998)*
◆ *Largest Crowd: 59,282 (September 16, 1979)*
◆ *Also known as Stade Olympique*
◆ *Nickname: The Big O*

Pacific Bell Park

THERE IS GOOD NEWS and bad news for the long-suffering Giants fans in San Francisco. The good news is that their team no longer plays in abysmal Candlestick Park. The bad news is that although Pac Bell is a wonderful new facility, it is subject to the same fierce winds that plagued Candlestick.

The Giants built Pac Bell with private funds. The new stadium is located in the China Basin section of downtown San Francisco, adjacent to the bay. The ballpark is situated so that fans sitting at club-level seats or view level have a marvelous view of the water. The right-field wall runs perpendicular to the bay, and beyond the wall is a 35-foot-wide promenade where fans can stand to watch the game and await long balls. The distance to the wall from home plate, a mere 307 feet, presents an inviting target for left-handed hitters. This section, called the Old Navy Splash Landing, is the most notable feature inside the ballpark. Beyond the promenade is only the deep blue bay, called Willie McCovey Cove, where guys in little motorboats drift, ready to fish out baseballs that clear the stadium.

The trade-off for this water view, the most beautiful in all of baseball, is exposure to the strong wind. Unlike Safeco Field in Seattle, which has Plexiglas installed behind the seats in the upper deck, fans here shiver, just as they did at the Stick. Were it not for the bone-chilling wind, Pac Bell might be the only major-league ballpark where fans might prefer sitting up top; the water isn't visible from field-level seats.

ELLIS BURKS "I guess one of the best things about it is the great view. You got forty thousand screaming fans every night, which is always a plus. It's a beautiful all-around ballpark. You got to like coming here playing, the excitement of it. You can't beat it."

Several features here pay homage to ballparks gone by: bullpens located in foul territory instead of beyond outfield walls; grass cut with no pattern in it; the brick wall behind home plate. And there are a couple of entertainment features, such a Coke-bottle slide for kids above the bleachers in left field.

Whatever the conditions, fans here cheer long and loud for the home team, without prompting from the scoreboard. But for the price of Plexiglas . . .

- ◆ *Home of the San Francisco Giants*
- ◆ *San Francisco, California: Second Street, King Street, Third Street, and China Basin*
- ◆ *Built 2000*
- ◆ *Opening Day: April 11, 2000*
- ◆ *Cost: $319 Million*
- ◆ *Seating Capacity: 40,800*
- ◆ *Largest Crowd: 40,930 (April 11, 2000)*
- ◆ *Replaced 3Com Park (Candlestick Park), 2000*

DIMENSIONS	LF	LCF	CF	RCF	RF
(2000)	339	382	399	421; 365	307

It's a great atmosphere, a fun place to

play with a packed house every night.

You couldn't ask for anything more.

— CALVIN MURRAY

JOE NATHAN "The one thing I've noticed is just as far as the ball carries. I'd say, you keep a ball down, if you keep it on the ground, it's very calm. But if you hit a ball in the air here—you can see the flags blowing up top—if you hit it good, it's going a pretty good way. It can become a good home-field advantage for us, with outfielders learning the wall. You got to learn certain fly balls, how they're going to bounce off the brick, if they're going to stick inside the fence."

J. T. SNOW "I think that this park, after playing for three years in Candlestick, is pretty unbelievable. As far as playing in front of ten or fifteen thousand a game, then you come here and you play in front of forty thousand. They did it right as far as making it not too big, not too small . . . There was a lot of talk about this being a hitter's ballpark. I don't think the ball's been flying out of here like people thought, especially to right field. I think it's pretty fair. So for guys who played in Candlestick, it's almost like going from the outhouse to the penthouse."

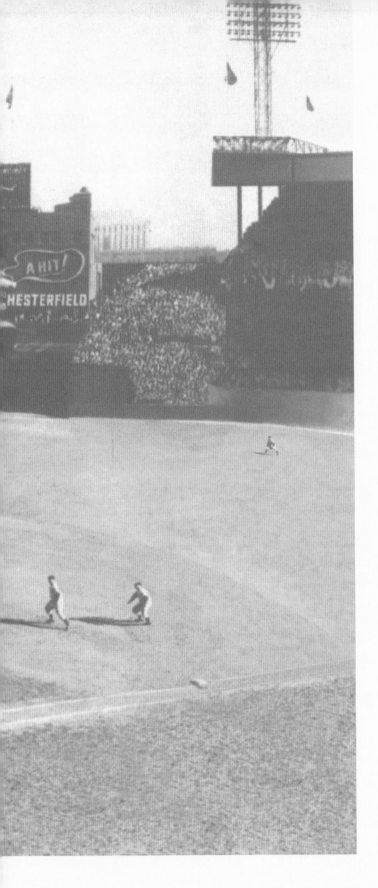

Polo Grounds

FROM 1903 UNTIL 1957, there were three Major League Baseball teams located in New York City: the Brooklyn Dodgers and New York Giants in the National League, and the New York Yankees in the American League. In the mid-fifties, the Dodgers' owners decided that their inner-city fan base was eroding, moving to the suburbs. They demanded that the city build a new stadium in the area where Shea Stadium now stands. When the city dragged its feet, the Dodgers cut a deal with Los Angeles and moved the franchise. It is speculated that the principal owner, Walter O'Malley, really wanted to move all along. He also persuaded the Giants to move to San Francisco. When the Dodgers and Giants departed for the 1958 season, that left the Yankees as the only team in the New York area.

Some New York fans chose to follow their teams from afar. Since there were very few televised ball games, however, it was difficult. Perhaps some of the disenchanted became Yankees fans. Maybe they stopped following baseball altogether. In any case, a definite void had been created that some said would never be filled. But in 1962, when the National League decided to expand and add a franchise in New York, a unique opportunity arose to root for a team that no one had ever cheered before: the New York Mets.

The Mets needed a temporary home while a new stadium was built, and they chose the former home of the New York Giants. Polo Grounds was located in Harlem, at the northern end of Manhattan, adjacent to the Harlem River and about a mile south of the George Washington Bridge. A quarter-mile south and across the river in the Bronx stood Yankee Stadium. Although these two ballparks stood in close geographical proximity, they were really worlds apart. Yankee Stadium was the most famous ballpark in the world, home of the Bronx

AL JACKSON "I thought it was such a unique ballpark because of the dimensions. It was like 250, 255 feet down the lines and God knows how far it was in center field. I loved pitching there. At the time, hitters were different than they are now. It'd be very easy for hitters to hit in that ballpark the way they hit now, because they hit to all fields. The majority of hitters then were pull hitters, so you kind of pitched away and made them hit the ball to the biggest part of the ballpark."

JEFF GREENFIELD (COMMENTATOR)
"When I was a kid, I was a Yankees fan. For some reason . . . my dad and I went to the Polo Grounds. Everything about it was strange. First of all, it was the wrong subway stop—155th. The colors on the wall, instead of the Yankee Stadium blue-and-white tile, they were orange and black. Couldn't understand that. And also, the Polo Grounds was an incredibly decrepit stadium. . . . It was huge—dead center field was 484 feet, I believe. And the players dressed in the clubhouse in center field and walked out. It was all green instead of blue, and I just remember thinking, Where am I? It was really like almost waking up in a dream where something isn't quite right. . . . Also, the dimensions of the Polo Grounds were the most neurotic of any ball field: 484 feet to dead center and 296 down the left-field line, and the actual right-field line—they didn't mark it because they were ashamed—was, like, 258 feet. . . . The walls were 20 feet high. All I remember about it was how odd it was. If you've been to one stadium only, your theory is, baseball's played in Yankee Stadium. And if you were a kid, you were a fan of one team. I think the only thing weirder would have been to go to a Yankees game in another American League ballpark and hear everybody root against them."

Bombers, the most successful sports franchise in history. Polo Grounds, abandoned by the Giants, stood dormant and in need of repair. The Mets spent a mere $250,000 to refurbish it, but this was a temporary fix. Their new home, Shea Stadium, would be ready in two years, in time for the 1964 season.

Polo Grounds was one of the more oddly configured ballparks. The distance down the foul lines was a mere pop fly away—280 feet to left field, 258 feet to right. But the center-field wall was a lengthy 475 feet from home plate, creating a horseshoe effect. The clubhouse was located beyond that fence, above the playing field, up a flight of stairs. Atop the clubhouse was the huge Rheingold beer sign (it was the Chesterfield cigarette sign when the Giants played there). Beneath the clubhouse on the field level were gates that opened at the end of the game, allowing fans to walk across the field to leave the park.

The first Mets game was scheduled against St. Louis for the evening of April 10, 1962, to be televised from St. Louis. It rained. New York's WOR-TV Channel 9 showed *Rainout Theater* instead, probably a portent for the season. The next night, the Mets lost 11–4 to the Cards. There were eight consecutive losses after that. By summer the Mets were firmly in last place.

On July 15, 1962, Polo Grounds became my first baseball stadium. The Mets rose to the occasion that hot Sunday, winning the first game of the twin bill 5–3 before dropping the nightcap 9–8. Few players stood out on that mostly losing team. There was Gil Hodges, a solid pro with the Brooklyn Dodgers for many years, but near the end of his playing career in 1962. But he wasn't at the park that day, having just undergone knee surgery. "Marvelous" Marv Throneberry was the most popular Met that year, as much for his misadventures in the field as for a few late-inning, game-winning home runs. Marv, aided by the New York press, came to symbolize the hopes and frustrations of Mets fans. With each base-running blunder and costly fielding mishap, his popularity grew. He batted once that July day and struck out. And Roger Craig, the staff ace, lost twenty-four games that year—he must have been pretty good if manager Casey Stengel kept trotting him out there.

The team would eventually lose 120 games that year, still an all-time record.

The Mets continued to be the doormat for the National League until 1969, when the Yankees' fortunes hit rock bottom and the Mets rose from ninth place the prior year to World Champions under the leadership of former player Gil Hodges. The eight years it took for the expansion team to become the champions were relatively brief, but at the time it seemed quite long. Few teams in history have played as poorly for as long as those Amazin' Mets. But for the fans who embraced the Mets from the beginning, it was worth the wait.

Polo Grounds was demolished shortly after the final game was played there on September 18, 1963. Like Ebbets Field in Brooklyn, apartment buildings were erected on the site. As Frank Sinatra sang, "There used to be a ballpark here . . ."

DON MUELLER "I signed with the Giants in 1944 with one year left in high school. Mel Ott was the manager, and he was my favorite ballplayer. That's why I wanted to play in the Polo Grounds. We had good groundskeepers. It was a beautiful old park with a fabulous history."

- *Former home of the New York Giants and the New York Mets*
- *New York City: Eighth Avenue, East 155th Street, Harlem River Drive, and East 157th Street*
- *Built 1911*
- *Opening Day: June 28, 1911 (New York Giants); April 13, 1962 (New York Mets)*
- *Seating Capacity: 55,987*
- *Largest Crowd: 60,747 (May 3, 1937)*
- *Before renovation in 1911, known as Brotherhood Park, 1890–1910*
- *Formerly known as Brush Stadium, 1911–1919*
- *Home of the National League New York Giants, 1891–1957*
- *Home of the American Football League New York Titans, 1962–1963*
- *Demolished 1963*

GEORGE PLIMPTON (AUTHOR) "I can remember the first sight of the inside of a great stadium. I was, I suppose, ten years old at the time, or nine . . . Cliff Melton was pitching for the New York Giants, it was the Giants versus the Yankees, and he had great big ears. But the thing I truly remember is that wonderful green symmetry of the stadium. It was going from the darkness of a tunnel into that amazing bright green world."

BOBBY THOMSON "My first workout [was] in the Polo Grounds while still in high school. The field felt like hallowed ground."

BOBBY BRAGAN "As a member of the Phillies . . . our first road game was against the Giants in the Polo Grounds. Bill Terry was the Giants manager. The size and shape of the Polo Grounds would impress anyone . . . One had to be impressed with the manicured look of the well-kept grounds, both the grass and dirt portion. It was a thrill indeed!"

DIMENSIONS	LF	LCF	CF	RCF	RF
	279 or 280*	447 or 455	475 or 483	440 or 450	258 or 259

Outfield wall markings varied from year to year.

First time I saw a major-league ballpark was the Polo Grounds, and I was maybe eight or nine years old and it was an absolute great treat. It was a unique ballpark and I ended up, although I was in Massachusetts, playing at the Polo Grounds when I was sixteen years old in a high school game. I remember it was all-encompassing. My first memory of a player was Willie Mays chasing down fly balls in batting practice; Leo Durocher hit the fly balls. It was just absolutely an amazing experience.

—FRAN HEALY

Pro Player Stadium

THIS STADIUM WAS FORMERLY known as Joe Robbie Stadium, after the late owner of the NFL's Miami Dolphins. The Marlins were an expansion team in 1993, owned by Wayne Huizenga, who purchased the stadium from the Robbie family and sold the naming rights to a sportswear company.

But by any name, this is a football facility. Joe Robbie Stadium was designed for the Dolphins, not for baseball's Marlins. Although not built until 1987, it followed the previous decade's trend of building multipurpose stadiums in the suburbs, and it is far removed from downtown Miami. Its size alone precludes this facility from being an ideal place to watch a baseball game. From foul line to foul line in the outfield, the entire upper deck is closed and covered by tarpaulins during regular-season baseball games, although these sections were opened for 1997 postseason play; and the rest of the upper-deck seats are quite high and far removed from the field. Lower-level seating also presents problems, particularly down the lines, where the configuration makes it difficult to follow the action. From some of these sections it is virtually impossible to see both home plate and the pitcher's mound.

Before the Marlins came into existence, it was assumed that the almost daily late-afternoon thunderstorms in Miami would cause countless rainouts. But while there are indeed many weather delays, there have not been as many postponements as originally feared. On the other hand, there is the often stifling humidity.

In 1997 the Marlins won the World Championship in just their

JASON KENDALL

"My first big-league game was in Florida, Joe Robbie Stadium . . . amazing. I grew up in a baseball family, my dad played in the big leagues. You know I'm living a dream. I wake up with a smile on my face every day, put a big-league uniform on, I get to walk into a big-league ballpark. Can't beat that."

When I enter that stadium it reminds

me of jungle gyms, like a playground

for kids, because of the colors.

—BILL SPIERS

- *Home of the Florida Marlins*
- *Miami, Florida: NW 199th Street, NW 27th Avenue, and NW 203rd Street*
- *Built 1987*
- *Opening Day: April 5, 1993*
- *Cost: $115 Million*
- *Seating Capacity (Baseball): 45,706 (1993); 41,855 (1998); 35,521 (2000)*
- *Largest Crowd: 67,494 (October 25, 1997)*
- *Home of NFL's Miami Dolphins*

DIMENSIONS	LF	LCF	CF	RCF	RF
(1993)	330	361	404	385	345
(1999)	330	385*	404	385	345

*Outfield corner in left center field is 434 feet.

GARY THORNE (BROADCASTER) "From a broadcast perspective, it's a very nice ballpark to work in. The broadcast booths are large and fairly close to home plate compared to some of the newer ballparks. The trouble is, it's a football field. The outfield seats, because they haven't been able to draw many people, you have the entire upper deck covered with canvas. You feel as though you start half-empty. It's also out in the middle of nowhere, which I think has really hurt them, because I don't think a lot of baseball fans will actually make the trek out there. Even in the year they won, they weren't drawing that well, and I think it was because of where the ballpark was located. From the fans' perspective, those who sit downstairs from the right- and left-field lines down to the plate have pretty good seats. There's a bit of an angle problem because the seats were put in for football, so they're not exactly angled in toward the field, and you kind of have to turn your head all the time. But it's not as bad as it is at some ballparks that are football fields. The weather has a huge impact: Generally you get your 5:00 P.M. to 7:00 P.M. ferocious thunderstorms that come rattling through there, so a lot of teams have trouble getting in their pregame activities. Visiting teams come in, first game, they like to get a feel for the field. And if you can't get out there for that first game, it affects how you play in the series."

fifth year of existence, the fastest of any expansion team. Much has been written about former owner Wayne Huizenga's checkbook champions and his subsequent dismantling and sale of the team. His effort to persuade the taxpayers to build a new stadium for the Marlins failed. In December 2000, new owner John Henry announced an agreement with the city of Miami to build a retractable-roof natural-grass baseball field downtown. The Marlins and the taxpayers will share in the cost of the new ballpark, scheduled to open in 2004. The team hopes that the location and intimate size of the stadium will recapture the excitement of the 1997 championship season.

DEREK BELL "They got a small Fenway in left field, a mini-monster, and it's very colorful; it's turquoise. It's a very bright stadium. Plus my family is down there to watch me play in that stadium."

Qualcomm Stadium

THIS BALLPARK used to be called Jack Murphy Stadium, named after a well-respected journalist who was instrumental in bringing Major League Baseball to San Diego. Referred to affectionately by locals as the Murph, it fell victim to the nineties trend of stadium naming rights. The name change, awkward though it may sound, is not as objectionable as another trend: enlarging what is already a multipurpose stadium. This ballpark was never an ideal baseball facility, with a huge scoreboard in right center field more suited for football, and with seats positioned at odd angles in many sections, reinforcing the off-center feeling.

The additional sections, built for the 1998 season, were erected on both sides of the scoreboard, enclosing the park and eliminating the view of the rolling hills and trees beyond. Luckily this did not change the climate here, which is among the most beautiful in the country. In fact, some people speculate that this languid atmosphere and laid-back lifestyle contribute to players losing some competitive edge. Since the Padres have won only two pennants in their thirty-plus years of existence, this theory may have merit.

The leisurely aura here stands in contrast to the longtime presence of Padre superstar Tony Gwynn. In an era of free agency and constant player movement, Gwynn has turned down more money to remain in San Diego. A fixture here since 1982, he goes about his business on the field with visible concentration and

MARK WOHLERS "When I first got called up, we were in San Diego. I think when I got to the major leagues, it was more meaningful because I knew I'd have a chance to perform on it, and I just realized how much bigger it is when you're in the stadium than when you're outside or watching it on TV."

TODD PRATT "It's peaceful, palm trees are nice in back of the fence. Seems like it's great weather every time I get in there."

JOSÉ VIZCAINO "September 10, 1989, San Diego, Jack Murphy Stadium—it was a dream come true: It was my first time in the big leagues."

You couldn't help but

just go, "Ahhhh…"

— **DAVID WELLS**

- *Home of the San Diego Padres*
- *San Diego, California: Stadium Way, Interstate 8, Murphy Canyon Road, and Friars Road*
- *Built 1967*
- *Opening Day: April 8, 1969*
- *Cost: $27 Million*
- *Seating Capacity: 50,000 (1968); 59,254 (1992); 46,510 (2000)*
- *Largest Crowd: 65,427 (October 21, 1998)*
- *Nickname: The Murph*
- *Original Name: San Diego Stadium*
- *Former Name: Jack Murphy Stadium*
- *Home of NFL's San Diego Chargers*

DIMENSIONS	LF	LCF	CF	RCF	RF
(1969)	330	375	420	375	330
(1991)	327	378	405	378	327
(2000)	327	370	405	368	330

ROBERTO ALOMAR "My first game was supposed to be in Los Angeles. It got postponed. When I went to Jack Murphy Stadium, that's where I started playing my first game. . . . It's amazing how different it is from the minor leagues to the big leagues. When you go into a big-league stadium, you look up, you see a lot of people, big stadium, nice fields, big scoreboard. Things you don't see in the minor leagues."

TOM PAGNOZZI "The first time I ever walked into a major-league stadium, I was probably eight or nine years old, in San Diego. The Padres. Growing up in Tucson, Arizona, we always vacationed in southern California. Every summer, Disneyland, do all that stuff, catch a ball game. And my dad was a Cubs fan. The first game I ever went to was a Padres-Cubs game in San Diego. You walked into it—from playing on the Little League field to that, I mean, you just could not imagine what it looked like. It looked like . . . a bunch of gold bars stacked up, it was just unbelievable. The grass was manicured. The infield, there was no bad hop. The batter's box was perfect. The grass looked like it just got cut in a different weave. It was incredible, absolutely incredible."

determination—a certain first-ballot Hall of Famer.

In November 1998, San Diego voters approved financing for a baseball-only ballpark. This new facility, to be built downtown, should continue the positive trend of old-looking new ballparks like Camden Yards and Jacobs Field, which are integrated into the community and are large enough to be comfortable but small enough to enhance the experience.

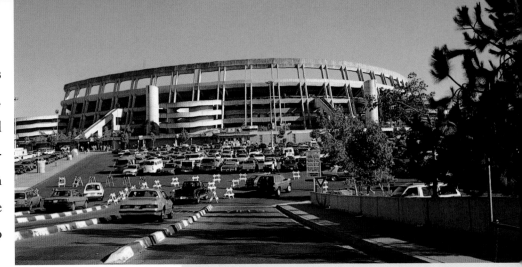

Rogers Centre

BILLED AS THE WORLD'S Greatest Entertainment Center, Toronto's Rogers Centre (known as Skydome until 2005) boasts an elaborate hotel and several restaurants, including the ubiquitous Hard Rock Café and numerous McDonald's scattered throughout the huge building. With its glitz and vast facilities, this is indeed no ordinary ballpark.

Like most domed stadiums, Rogers Centre has the usual nonpastoral characteristics such as bright green artificial turf and a roof. However, this roof retracts, and unlike its cousin in Montreal, it really works, albeit not as quickly as the roof at Bank One Ballpark in Phoenix. About a half hour before game time on days when the weather cooperates, the dome begins to open, folding into itself in several sections in less than twenty minutes. The contrast between

closed and open is striking. Batting practice takes place in the artificially lit gloom, punctuated by the odd plink of the ball off the wooden bats, with the air's stillness creating a warehouse effect. Then the roof opens to create an outdoor ballpark, with the sense of spaciousness, the sky above, the unique sound of horsehide meeting ash, the sound dispersing rather than echoing off the dome.

The sight lines at Rogers Centre are not among the best in baseball: It is difficult to see the batter, the wild pitches, or foul pops behind the catcher from

160

JOHN OLERUD "The first big-league stadium that I was at as a player was the Skydome. And that was also a pretty big deal at the time, with the retractable roof and everything. When I signed with the Blue Jays and was there in Toronto, it was a big thrill because this is something that I'd been working for ever since I was a kid and always hoped to make it, but never really knew for sure if I would make it or not."

MICHAEL KAY (BROADCASTER) "Skydome is underrated, I think, because of all the retro ballparks. It has everything you would want as a fan. The concessions are great, it's great working conditions, good clubhouses, great press box. It was the first retractable-roof stadium. I always refer to it as 'Baseball and the Jetsons.'"

MEL STOTTLEMYRE "When it was built, it was one of the completely different domes. It was full most of the time. They're suffering a little bit now attendance-wise. The field itself is very fast, and when the roof is closed you do get that feeling that you are in an enclosed stadium. I think most of the visiting teams prefer the roof to be open."

PAT GILLICK (GENERAL MANAGER) "A fall afternoon at Skydome in 1992, after a victory parade through the streets of Toronto, the team players, their families, and forty-five thousand plus fans gathered inside the stadium. An electricity emanated from each person on the field and in the stands: It was excitement, pride, joy over the first World Series win in the history of that franchise."

- *Home of the Toronto Blue Jays*
- *Toronto, Ontario: Front Street, Peter Street, and Bremner Boulevard*
- *Built 1989*
- *Opening Day: June 5, 1989*
- *Cost: $500 Million*
- *Seating Capacity: 50,516 (1989); 51,000 (1998)*
- *Largest Crowd: 52,382 (All-Star Game, July 9, 1991)*
- *Former Name: Skydome, 1989-2005*
- *Replaced Exhibition Stadium, 1989*
- *First Major League Baseball stadium to draw 4 million fans in one season (4,001,526 in 1991)*

DIMENSIONS	LF	LCF	CF	RCF	RF
(1991)	328	375	400	375	328

the first dozen or so rows above home plate. The upper deck is one of the highest of any stadium. And field-level seats are not without problems, particularly in the outfield, where the rows are narrow, seats are crammed together, and the shallow incline makes it difficult to watch the action.

During the early nineties the Blue Jays sold out virtually every game here, and became the first franchise to draw more than 4 million fans in a season. But Toronto has not fielded a strong contender since winning two World Championships, in 1992 and 1993, and attendance has dropped commensurately. But at least there have been no cries for a new ballpark.

	EVENT	SUBJECT TO THE CONDITIONS ON THE BACK HEREOF
B55 M3	B55	SUN AUG 2,1992 1:35PM SKYDOME NO REFUNDS * NO EXCHANGES
103 AISLE	ONE ADMISSION	TORONTO BLUE JAYS VS NEW YORK YANKEES
7 ROW	$3.50 PRICE INCL. FED. AND PROV. TAXES	

90613 GATE 5 848670
11 2/15 103 7 11 $13.50
SEAT AISLE ROW SEAT ADMISSION

When you were a little kid and that stadium was brand-new, it was awesome. And it's still awesome.

—DARYLE WARD

Safeco Field

THEY SAY YOU CAN'T JUDGE a book by its cover, and that old saying is proven here in Seattle. Driving up to this stadium, just across from where the Kingdome stood, you might wonder why they bothered imploding the old stadium at all: The outward appearance of Safeco is similar to a warehouse or an airplane hangar under construction. Inside, though, this stadium shines.

Reminiscent of the similar retractable domes at Bank One Ballpark in Arizona and Enron Field in Houston, Safeco is two different places, depending on whether or not the roof is open. With the roof shut, this is arena baseball, albeit with natural grass. But when the roof opens, weather permitting, the difference is stunning. The outfield is totally enclosed, so fans sitting in the lower deck do not get a skyline view, but the upper deck features a marvelous vista of downtown Seattle. And Safeco boasts perhaps the best fan feature in all of baseball: a Plexiglas shield that surrounds the upper deck behind the seats and cuts down the wind to almost nothing. Stadiums located near water, like Shea Stadium in New York and Pacific Bell Park in San Francisco, can be quite uncomfortable when cold winds blow early or late in the season. Not so at Safeco.

Overall, fewer old-time features have been incorporated here than in some other new ballparks—the main scoreboard, for example, displays out-of-town scores electronically, not via hand operation—but compared to the Kingdome, this is baseball nirvana.

The Kingdome was a dump.

Safeco is spacious,

fan-friendly, and the roof

is an interesting aspect.

— MARK MCLEMORE

EDGAR MARTINEZ "It's more like a pitcher's type of park. It's bigger than the King-dome, there's more room in the outfield. But the ball, on differ-ent days, it travels differently. Mostly it doesn't travel as well as it did in the Kingdome."

ALEX RODRIGUEZ "I love this stadium. It has a great infield, it has a fan-friendly atmosphere, and the amenities in here, they're just gorgeous. To me, it's in the top three fields in the world . . . This is the way baseball should be played, outdoors on natural grass."

JAY BUHNER "I think it's a very fan-friendly, great environ-ment. It shows the cityscape, so aesthetically it's a beautiful ball-park. It's something that this city and community wanted to have, which is baseball outside, real grass and all the smells of baseball."

DAN WILSON "I love it. It's a beautiful ballpark, there's no doubt about it. They did a great job mak-ing it fan-friendly. This part of the country has a beau-tiful summertime, and this park can certainly take advantage of that. Saturday and Sunday, the sun's out, the roof's open, there's really no place like it in America."

◆ *Home of the Seattle Mariners*

◆ *Seattle, Washington: Royal Brougham Way, First Avenue South, South Atlantic Street, and Third Avenue South*

◆ *Built 1999*

◆ *Opening Day: July 15, 1999*

◆ *Cost: $517 Million*

◆ *Seating Capacity: 47,145*

◆ *Largest Crowd: 48,010 (October 6, 2000)*

◆ *Replaced the Kingdome, 1999*

DIMENSIONS	LF	LCF	CF	RCF	RF
(2000)	331	388	405	385	326

Shea Stadium

THE NEW YORK METS played at Polo Grounds in 1962 and 1963 while Shea was being built across the street from the site of the 1964 New York World's Fair. The hope was that visitors to the fair would be drawn to the park by mere proximity. But more important was that Shea was located between two major highways and amid the rapidly expanding communities in Queens and the Long Island suburbs.

Shea was not the first park constructed with the suburbs in mind (that was Milwaukee's County Stadium, in 1953), but it was recognized at the time as the ideal stadium of the future. Accessible from major roads, with plenty of parking, Shea acknowledged the reality of urban flight: If fans were moving out of cities, baseball teams would have to follow them. This trend continued for thirty years, until 1993, when Camden Yards was built in the downtown Inner Harbor of Baltimore.

Shea's location, while convenient for suburbanites, also has its drawbacks. First is weather: The ballpark is open in the outfield and quite close to Flushing Bay, and cold winds can make it extremely uncomfortable, especially in April and October. In a futile attempt to moderate the wind chill, the city of San Francisco enclosed the outfield at Candlestick Park. There was talk of enclosing Shea with a dome, but the cost was deemed prohibitive and the project was dropped. Plans to replace Shea with a new stadium are on hold.

The other major problem is its location adjacent to La Guardia Airport, making it perhaps the noisiest stadium in baseball. Games are frequently delayed while jets roar overhead. During the two weeks when the U.S. Open tennis tournament is played across the street at the National Tennis Center, planes are rerouted during matches. No such accommodation is made for the Mets.

TUG MCGRAW "My dreams about becoming a Major League Baseball player . . . came true later at Shea Stadium in New York, when I walked onto Shea Stadium in my Mets uniform for the first time and felt like I was the luckiest guy in the world. Because every day when I came to work for the Mets, I would go to Shea Stadium, play big-league baseball. And then after the game, walk across the street and go to the World's Fair. It was just too good to be true."

WILLIE RANDOLPH "I never got into any of the good seats, mostly the cheap seats, but [was] just totally mesmerized by the aura of the field and the history behind some of these ballparks. My uncle would drive me down to the Grand Central Parkway, leaving Shea Stadium, and I remember looking out the rear window and I would say to myself, 'I'm going to be there one day. I'm gonna play in that stadium one day' . . . And it came true for me."

ERIC YOUNG "The first time was when I went to Shea Stadium to see the Mets. I was in the nosebleed seats way up there, and they used to hit pop-ups and you think it's coming to you, and the ball wouldn't be close to me, it'd be either on the field or in the first section. And I just remember always wanting to get a ball. And I felt like all the players heard me and knew that I was up there cheering for them. And that was a thrill."

PHIL GARNER "In 1964 my family and I traveled to New York City for the World's Fair. The grounds were across from the ballpark. We wandered over to the stadium and it happened to be open, so we walked in. As a freshman in high school, my dream was to play professional baseball. As I stood at home plate, the stands towered above like nothing the small east Tennessee country boy had ever seen. I told my mom and dad, 'Someday I'll play here.' My first year in the big leagues with the Oakland A's we played in Shea because Yankee Stadium was being renovated. Dreams do come true."

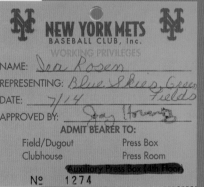

[Shea] was a lot better than being in the minor leagues.

—KEVIN MITCHELL

- *Home of the New York Mets*
- *Flushing, New York: 126th Street and Roosevelt Avenue*
- *Built 1964*
- *Opening Day: April 17, 1964*
- *Cost: $28.5 Million*
- *Seating Capacity: 55,000 (1964); 55,601 (1986); 56,521 (2000)*
- *Largest Crowd: 57,397 (October 17, 1969)*
- *Formal Name: William A. Shea Municipal Stadium*
- *Former home of NFL's New York Jets*

DIMENSIONS	LF	LCF	CF	RCF	RF
(1964)	330	371	410	371	330
(1992)	341	371	410	371	341
(1999)	338	371	410	371	338

MO VAUGHN "First stadium I ever saw: Shea Stadium . . . It just seemed so enormous to me. I knew that this is the big leagues, this is what it's all about, what you work for all your life. But I think that the size of stadiums, the fact that people are actually coming out, paying to watch you play, is what you think about. And the excitement of it is a great thing."

Sportsman's Park

IN THE EARLY SIXTIES, when I discovered baseball, this ballpark was named Busch Stadium, after the family who owned the St. Louis Cardinals and Anheuser Busch. When the new stadium was built in 1966, it was named Busch Memorial Stadium, but was almost always referred to as Busch Stadium. To avoid confusion, most people now refer to the original Busch Stadium as Sportsman's Park.

The Busch family sold the Cardinals in the late nineties, and it's hard to believe that there is no family involvement with the team that is synonymous with them in the Gateway City.

RED SCHOENDIENST "In them days . . . there was no television, so you had no chance unless you saw a picture in the paper or something. But the first [stadium] I saw was old Sportsman's Park when we came in for a tryout. Never saw a big-league game, but they had a piece in the paper where you could try out. That was back in 1942. Me and two other guys from the little town [of] Germantown, we came in and tried out and to look at it, to see it and everything, it was quite a thrill . . . to see all the big-leaguers like Terry Moore, Slaughter, and Marion, and all them guys. Cooper boys, Pepper Martin. Dizzy Dean. I was gonna play. Give me a chance and see if I could make it. And it wasn't but a year and a half and I did play, after I went in the service and come back."

CHRIS CHAMBLISS "My first recollection was when I was a child. My father took me to old Sportsman's Park in St. Louis, the old stadium, and that was the first time I remember being in a ballpark. I forget where we sat; we were up in the upper deck somewhere and it . . . was just like magic. It's like something out of a dream, where you just see a ball field like that. I've always loved being around the ballpark, but Sportsman's Park was the first place I remember."

JERRY REUSS "First Major League Baseball stadium that I saw in person was old Busch Stadium in St. Louis. And my first impression was walking up the ramp. I could smell all the old cigar smoke, the stale beer that had been there for years that was a trademark of old ballparks. But the biggest impression that was left to me was all of the green grass. I'd never seen so much green grass that was perfectly tailored."

ENOS SLAUGHTER ". . . 1938, join the Gashouse Gang, the park: Sportsman's, St. Louis. Was great to get a chance to play in the majors."

GARY GAETTI "The first big-league ballpark I saw was Sportsman's Park, St. Louis. It was hard to see the whole field because I think we ended up sitting behind a pillar, a post, or something like that . . . But I liked the whole scene. My most vivid memory of coming to the ballpark was the aroma . . . the smell of the beer, the stale beer and the hot dogs that were being cooked and the hamburgers. I think at that time you could smoke in the stadium . . . When I come back here, I'll smell those same smells and have one of those warm, fuzzy moments, you know? I'll smell that now and I'll remember how vivid that was to me at that time when I was nine and ten years old."

JOE GARAGIOLA JR. (GENERAL MANAGER) "My most vivid memories, early memories, are of the old Sportsman's Park or Busch Stadium. It was actually called Busch Stadium in the fifties, and I vividly recall the Anheuser Busch sign over left center field. And then there was a clock mounted on one of the light towers in right center field, and I recall one night Duke Snider hit it and it was like *The Natural*; it was the neon tubing exploding."

BOB CARPENTER (BROADCASTER) "I grew up in St. Louis, which is an unbelievable baseball town, and I remember when I was a little guy, my dad took me to Busch Stadium, which is the old ballpark. It was Sportsman's Park up until 1953, when Anheuser Busch bought it; then it became Busch Stadium. But that's where the Cardinals played from '53 through the first part of '66. And the thing that I remember most vividly, from the first time my dad took me to the ballpark, was coming up the street and still being a couple of blocks away from the ballpark and seeing those lights; the old ballparks had just the tallest light standards. And when I walked into that ballpark, into the seats, to see that green field all lit up at night. And Stan Musial hitting the ball up on·the pavilion in right field; and we had Kenny Boyer, Curt Flood, and Bob Gibson—so this would have been in the late fifties. It was an unbelievable impression that made on me. But the first thing I ever remember about a major-league ballpark was seeing those lights, you know, from a couple of blocks away as we drove up into north St. Louis."

- *Former home of the St. Louis Cardinals*
- *St. Louis, Missouri: Dodier Street, Spring Street, Sullivan Avenue, and Grand Avenue*
- *Built 1909*
- *Opening Day: April 14, 1909 (St. Louis Browns)*
- *Final Game: May 8, 1966*
- *Seating Capacity: 17,600 (1909); 25,000 (1912); 30,500 (1934)*
- *Largest Crowd: 45,770 (July 12, 1931)*
- *Also known as Busch Stadium, 1953–1966*
- *Former home of the American League St. Louis Browns, 1909–1953*
- *Replaced by Busch Memorial Stadium, 1966*

DIMENSIONS	LF	LCF	CF	RCF	RF
(1909)	368	379	430	354	335
(1942)	351	379	420	354	309

TIM MCCARVER "My first experience in a major-league ballpark was as a ten-year-old Little Leaguer visiting Sportsman's Park in St. Louis. I had my picture taken with Eddie Stanky then, and Eddie was one of three people to whom I dedicated my recent book. He taught me how to play the game, think the game, and ultimately how to talk the game."

BOB BROEG (AUTHOR) "I'm a writer, not a poet, but I honestly don't believe I've seen bluer blue than the sky, greener green than the grass, or milkier white [than that] of the dry-cleaned home uniforms that Memorial Day 1927 when, age nine, I saw the World Champion Cardinals play for the first time—and sweep a doubleheader from Cincinnati. It was the seventy-five-cent right-field pavilion at St. Louis's Sportsman's Park, where the closest to me with the black-circled "World Champions" around a ringed Redbird on his left breast was a man I'd get to know better, Billy Southworth. I don't think heaven can be much nicer than the moment I burst up the steps to the point where I could see the sky, the grass, and the clean uniform of the Cardinals, fresh off a trip and already at home in my heart."

DEWAYNE STAATS (BROADCASTER) "I was a kid, went in there for a night game against the Milwaukee Braves, and I remember the banks of lights on that grass in the outfield made the whole setting seem surreal. You'd walk out, it was on Grand Avenue in kind of a borderline area of town on the north side in St. Louis. And you'd walk by there, you'd go down the sidewalk, and you'd have gum stuck to the sidewalk and all that. But you'd walk in that ballpark, it was like a different planet."

ERNIE BROGLIO "Being from the West Coast, I never had the pleasure of seeing a major-league park. So for me to go to St. Louis and see my first major-league park was a thrill and a half. I guess the forty thousand people in the stands, as compared to maybe two or three thousand people in the stands in minor-league baseball, has a lot to do with the excitement . . . Just the size of these parks is awesome."

JERRY LUMPE "My first time seeing a big-league park was Sportsman's Park in St. Louis, and it was heaven. I had heard the games on radio by Harry Caray and Gabby Street, but to actually set foot in the park, see the green grass, hear the sound of the bat hitting the ball reverberate all around me, is something I shall never forget. The new generic concrete stadiums can never replace those wonderful old metal-seat parks."

Three Rivers Stadium

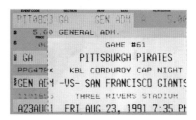

TONY WOMACK "I got called up in '93. It was Three Rivers, so that was my first. Just playing in front of so many people was probably the best memory I can think of. I grew up in Virginia, so I never went to a major-league game until I actually played here."

MIKE TORREZ "What I remember is that when it rained there, there were the longest delays. Because it was a different type of AstroTurf that they used, it was more like a carpet—it took the longest time for them to squeeze it out, with all the run-off. I hated when it rained at Three Rivers—that's what it was when it rained there: a river."

SHANE ANDREWS
"My first time was in Pittsburgh at Three Rivers Stadium. I was a rookie and it was the first time I'd ever been to a big-league baseball game. It was overwhelming to me, just amazing."

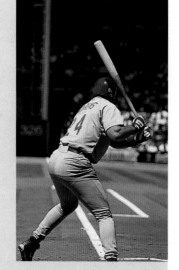

JAY JOHNSTONE
"Great place for a hitter. Good park to see in and the fences weren't very deep. For me, playing with the Phillies against the Pirates, we always had that controversial 'Who's the best in Pennsylvania?' In 1975, we went in there with a chance to beat them and maybe win the division, but they beat us in a doubleheader."

THREE RIVERS STADIUM was named for its location, at the confluence of the Ohio, Allegheny, and Monongahela Rivers, a picturesque area with a pastoral park adjacent to the stadium. Inside, however, this was another of the basic multipurpose, cookie-cutter concrete bowls built in the seventies to accommodate football crowds. Happily, PNC Park replaced Three Rivers in 2001.

In January 1993, the Pirates decided to block off approximately 11,000 seats in the upper deck, covering them with gray tarpaulins that pictured the teams' championship banners. According to a Pirates spokesman at the time, this "will make Three Rivers more intimate and baseball-oriented." It didn't. Like the other stadiums of its type, there was no sense of neighborhood, except perhaps for the last twenty rows of the upper deck, from which the tall buildings of downtown Pittsburgh were visible. Nothing was visible elsewhere in Three Rivers but concrete, artificial turf, and usually thousands of empty seats.

Every ballpark utilizes some device to get the crowd involved and cheering, whether it's the tomahawk chop, a hyperactive organist, or simply rhythmic applause. In Pittsburgh, a wonderful cartoon video of a locomotive blowing its whistle was played on the scoreboard. The fans clapped and cheered, stomping their feet in rhythm with the gathering speed of the train.

Despite winning World Championships in 1960 and 1979 and fielding consistently fine teams in the late eighties and early nineties, the Pirates have never drawn large numbers. Perhaps the low attendance is due to the relatively small population here or the fact that Pittsburgh is truly a football town. But the new PNC Park has the smallest seating capacity of any of the new stadiums, and it is hoped that enough fans will attend games to fill the house.

- ◆ *Former home of the Pittsburgh Pirates*

- ◆ *Pittsburgh, Pennsylvania: Stadium Circle and General Robinson Street*

- ◆ *Built 1970*

- ◆ *Opening Day: July 16, 1970*

- ◆ *Final Game: October 1, 2000*

- ◆ *Cost: $55 Million*

- ◆ *Seating Capacity: 50,500 (1970); 58,729 (1990); 47,972 (1993); 48,044 (2000)*

- ◆ *Largest Crowd: 57,533 (October 10, 1991)*

- ◆ *Home of NFL's Pittsburgh Steelers*

- ◆ *Site of the first World Series night game, October 13, 1971*

- ◆ *Demolished 2001*

JIM BOUTON "I hate it today, I hated it back then. I walked into the stadium, I said, 'This is stupid.' A sugar bowl with a baseball field in it. A baseball field is essentially square and you put a square into a circle and what do you have? Large half-moons of wasted space. I'm not surprised to see them tear these places down. They're not even good for football."

DIMENSIONS	LF	LCF	CF	RCF	RF
(1970)	340	385	410	385	340
(1991)	335	375	400	375	335

Tiger
Stadium

THERE IS A NEW BALLPARK in Detroit, Comerica Park, which means Tiger Stadium will be demolished, even though people here have worked tirelessly to save it. It was one of the four remaining old major-league ballparks, along with Fenway Park, Wrigley Field, and Yankee Stadium. Before it was replaced, Tiger Stadium shared with Fenway the claim of oldest ballpark in baseball, having made its debut in 1912. One could say it was even older: The site was also the home of Bennett Park, a wooden structure built in 1900. When that field could no longer be expanded to accommodate the increasing crowds, owner Frank Navin tore down the building and replaced it with a concrete-and-steel edifice, which he named for himself. The ballpark later underwent some renovations and a few name changes, but it always remained among the five or six best places to watch a major-league game.

The stands behind home plate were so close to the field that the screen, which protects fans from being struck by foul balls, extended all the way up to the roof. The only distant seats were in the outfield bleachers, and even those didn't seem all that far from the action. Sure, it was a bit crowded underneath the stands, and there wasn't much parking. But the history here, the emotional zeitgeist connecting generations of baseball fans, cannot be replaced.

185

JOHN SMOLTZ "When you're in the big leagues, you never get the chance to go sit in the stands too often. You get your perspective from the dugout, and it's totally different. The game changes when you're in the stands, so it's really all about perspective when you're used to the same routine—sitting in the dugout, watching the ball at angles that you watch . . . versus what the fans watch. I have a lot of memories [of Tiger Stadium]. It's unique. It's not one of your most glamorous stadiums, but it has a lot of tradition."

JIM KAAT "In 1946, my dad took me to see a weekday doubleheader between the Tigers and the Red Sox on a Wednesday afternoon, forty-some thousand people. When I walked in—at the time it was called Briggs Stadium—it was the greenest green and the uniforms were the whitest white that I had ever seen. I just thought it was a magnificent experience to see the color come alive from not having color television and only hearing games on radio."

F. P. SANTANGELO "I went to Tiger Stadium when I was seven years old, walked through the gate, saw the field, and I knew what I wanted to do the rest of my life. I was in the upper deck and John Hiller threw me a baseball, a left-handed relief pitcher for the Tigers, my very first big-league game."

RICO BROGNA "I'd say for me the most memorable place was Tiger Stadium, when I walked in there the first day I was called up to the major leagues. I actually got there about ten in the morning for a seven o'clock night game, but I just wanted to sit there and take it all in. I remember, first thing I thought was 'This place is like a palace or cathedral.' And the green grass was very green. It was very well manicured. It was just the color of the grass and the smell of the stadium and everything, the whole atmosphere was breathtaking."

- ◆ *Former home of the Detroit Tigers*
- ◆ *Detroit, Michigan: Michigan Avenue, National Avenue, Kaline Drive, and Trumbull Avenue*
- ◆ *Built 1912*
- ◆ *Opening Day: April 20, 1912*
- ◆ *Final Game: September 27, 1999*
- ◆ *Cost: $500,000*
- ◆ *Seating Capacity: 23,000 (1912); 52,416 (1989)*
- ◆ *Largest Crowd: 58,369 (July 20, 1947)*
- ◆ *Known as Navin Field, 1912–1937*
- ◆ *Known as Briggs Stadium, 1938–1960*
- ◆ *Former home of NFL's Detroit Lions*
- ◆ *Replaced by Comerica Park, 2000*

DIMENSIONS	LF	LCF	CF	RCF	RF
(1992)	340	365	440	370	325

DAVE CAMPBELL (BROADCASTER) "I was about eight years old and my dad took me to Tiger Stadium. I walked inside there and I mean the field was green, the seats were green, it was—I don't think Disneyland was in existence in those days, but to me, that was about as close to going to Disneyland. I thought I was in a Magic Kingdom."

JIM EDMONDS "My first big-league memory was coming into Tiger Stadium. It was the first day I got called up. I remember getting off the freeway in a taxicab and seeing it from the outside. It was probably the most impressive moment in my life."

HOWIE ROSE (BROADCASTER) "Tiger Stadium, to me, epitomizes what all the old ballparks were about: intimacy, charm, and a certain distinct ballpark aroma. The ambience of that ballpark takes you back to your youth, whether you grew up in Detroit or not. I was only there to do a few games three years ago. The thing I'll remember most was having been warned, thankfully, by Gary Cohen to bring a glove. Obviously, it wasn't from the standpoint of catching a foul ball and taking it home like I would when I was a kid. It was self-preservation. As soon as I got into that [broadcast] booth, the first foul ball that came back our way, I looked for [Fran] Healy, my partner—this guy caught in the big leagues—and he's gone. He's out the door, he's nowhere in sight, and I'm pounding my mitt. So it was the confluence of two dreams: to play in the big leagues and to broadcast in the big leagues. Because I'm actually sitting there with my headset on and the microphone on, broadcasting a game while I'm pounding my mitt, doing everything but calling the pitches."

DAN OKRENT (AUTHOR) "My father took me to my first baseball game in 1954 when I was six years old. This was in Briggs Stadium in Detroit, and I was overwhelmed by how green it all was, a green both comforting and thrilling. That has traveled with me to every baseball park I have ever visited. No color could possibly warm me more than this one."

SPARKY ANDERSON "The first stadium I ever saw was Briggs Stadium in Detroit, and I couldn't believe how big it was. I was seventeen years old and played the American Legion tournament there."

HOBIE LANDRITH "Having grown up in Detroit and having caught batting practice for the Tigers when I was fifteen, it was such a thrill to pick up a handful of dirt and remember the great catchers who played on this same diamond—Mickey Cochrane, Paul Richards, Birdie Tebbetts. Briggs Stadium, as it was known then, was a field of dreams for me, and I thank God my dream was realized."

HANK GREENWALD (BROADCASTER) "My first time in a baseball stadium was in my native Detroit at Briggs Stadium in 1943. I guess I was awed by how big the field looked. I'd never seen so much grass in my young life. The Tigers played the Philadelphia Athletics that day, and I remember seeing this tall man in a business suit standing on the steps of the dugout. It was Connie Mack, the manager. My other recollection of that day was watching the newspaper photographers who were down on the field during the game and would follow runners around the bases to get shots of them sliding in. They actually ran after them, lugging their cameras and wearing fedoras."

DAVE RIGHETTI "[Tiger Stadium] was a little bit of a nightmare for the Yankees in the eighties. Mostly because of the way it was built. In the locker room, the lockers are about a foot wide, guys are always bumping into each other. Going in the tunnel to the dugout, you're ducking the whole way. When you get to the dugout, you can't stand up straight. If you're a bullpen guy, there was this thing we called the Submarine. Basically, it was an underground concrete pit, a pillbox. You sit down in this hole and you can just barely peek out to see the game. You felt claustrophobic when you went to Detroit."

STEVE PHILLIPS (METS GENERAL MANAGER) "On my last day of second grade in June of 1971, I came home and began my summer vacation with the chicken pox. My parents had planned an end-of-the-school-year treat for myself and two of my brothers that included us going to Tiger Stadium for free Bat Day. Because of the chicken pox, I was not able to attend that game and obviously was very distraught. Luckily for me, in order to make up for this tremendous disappointment, my father was able to get two tickets to the All-Star game, which was being held in July at Tiger Stadium. As I recall, we were sitting in the upper deck in right field and it was an absolutely beautiful evening. We got there early enough for batting practice, and the players were launching balls into the stands regularly. When the game began, the most memorable event that evening was sitting in the upper deck when Reggie Jackson came to the plate and hit that remarkable home run that hit the light standards on top of the right-field roof. I still recall watching the ball come our way, as many had during batting practice, but yet keep going and going and going, and then losing sight of it as it went on top of the roof, over our heads. As I think back to that day, I can't help but feel glad that I had the chicken pox on the last day of school."

Tropicana Field

IN 1990, THREE YEARS before the Florida Marlins began their existence in Miami, a concrete domed stadium was built in the Tampa–St. Petersburg area on the west coast of Florida with the intention of attracting Major League Baseball. The area failed to lure an existing team such as the Chicago White Sox or Pittsburgh Pirates, but it did receive an expansion franchise for the 1998 season.

This stadium, initially called the Florida Suncoast Dome, cost the taxpayers $138 million but stood mostly dormant for seven years while hosting occasional tractor pulls, concerts, and the like. An additional $70 million was needed in renovations to prepare the place for baseball. Even then, the Major League Baseball mandate of natural-grass-only new stadiums had to be bypassed in order to bring baseball to this area at long last.

Tropicana Field, named for the orange juice company in another of the increasingly prevalent naming-rights deals, most closely resembles Minnesota's Metrodome. This domed ballpark is smaller than most of its cousins. The color of the roof, while dark enough to allow fly balls to be seen by fielders, is lighter than the old domes at Olympic Stadium and Kingdome. But light and airy this stadium is not, and there is no substitute for blue skies above.

The distance to the left-field foul pole is a mere 315 feet, making this an ideal ballpark for right-handed power hitters. In the lower deck, there is scarcely a bad seat to be found. At Tropicana, a few rows back between home plate and the

WORKING MEDIA

TAMPA BAY DEVIL RAYS
1998 Daily Pass

Name IRA ROSEN

Affiliation STADIUM VIEWS

Date 6/19/98

ADMIT TO:
Press Box
Pre-Game Field

Roving Grandstand
Clubhouse
Press Lounge

ADMIT BEARER THRU PRESS ENTRANCE/GATE 4

Andrew Maraniss
AUTHORIZATION

BOBBY SMITH "I think the first time you play in a stadium is the most exciting time that you have 'cause you're there, live. You hear all the hype and the hoopla about the stadium, but once you get there, I think you really look around and admire . . . how it really is up in the big leagues. My first big-league game was at Tropicana Stadium. I enjoy playing here, I like the atmosphere. The fans are great, and I'm having fun."

dugouts are luxury seats with video monitors attached. It seems odd that these fans sitting so close to the field that they can see pitchers throwing with remarkable velocity, then changing speeds with their pitches—subtleties visible only from such proximity—choose to watch screens instead.

Above the field are girders and catwalks that support the fixed-dome roof. Some of these obstructions are within reach of batted balls, and as a result, the architecture has affected the outcome of games, turning doubles into homers and homers into doubles.

A new artificial surface called Field Turf has been installed at Tropicana. This surface looks and plays more like real grass than AstroTurf. It's an improvement but nothing compared to green grass and a retractable dome.

- *Home of the Tampa Bay Devil Rays*
- *St. Petersburg, Florida: Central Avenue, 16th Street North, Dunmore Avenue, and 11th Street South*
- *Built 1990*
- *Opening Day: March 31, 1998*
- *Cost: $138 Million (1990)*
- *Renovation Cost (1998): $70 Million*
- *Seating Capacity: 45,000; 42,531 (2000)*
- *Largest Crowd: 45,369 (April 1, 1998)*
- *Original Name: Florida Suncoast Dome (1990)*
- *Former Name: Thunderdome (1996)*

DIMENSIONS	LF	LCF	CF	RCF	RF
(2000)	315	370	404	370	322

JIM PARQUE "Greg Vaughn hit a fly ball off me and it hit the second catwalk and they called it a home run. It's supposed to hit the third one. So that was ridiculous. The ball flies out of there, too. I think even I could hit a home run out of there."

VON JOSHUA "I think the situation in Tropicana Field is a little out of the ordinary with the catwalk up there. All the years I've been in baseball, I've seen ballparks with little quirks and different things. But nothing up in the sky like that . . . It just changes the whole complexion of a lot of ball games."

RICK WHITE "It was not a friendly pitcher's park. The fences were real short, so they had to move them back another ten feet. The ball carries pretty good due to the fact that it's a dome with the air-conditioning. It's a beautiful facility—they keep it real clean. The new turf, nobody else has anything like it. It's an all-dirt infield, which a lot of the infielders say they don't like because the bounces change coming off the turf."

BUBBA TRAMMELL "Playing at Tropicana Field, I liked the field and I liked what they did with the new turf, but the catwalks come into play way too much. I don't think they can do anything about the catwalks, though."

Turner Field

ORIGINALLY CONSTRUCTED for the 1996 Olympic Games, the city of Atlanta and the Braves did a good job reconfiguring an 80,000-seat multipurpose facility into a 50,000-seat baseball stadium.

The Ted, as it is called by fans of the Braves (for owner Ted Turner), is certainly an improvement over its predecessor, Fulton County Stadium, which was razed soon after the completion of this ballpark. But Turner Field is not quite on a par with Camden Yards and Jacobs Field, the two ballparks to which it is most often compared. Located about a mile from downtown Atlanta, it doesn't quite evoke the neighborhood ambience so prevalent in Baltimore and Cleveland, and it isn't quite as intimate and unique inside.

The lower-deck seats are within a reasonable distance of the playing field, though most fans down here are season-ticket holders. And the upper deck features views of the downtown skyline (which the lower deck does not), as well as the Coca-Cola Skyfield, a standing-room section in the highest part of left field, featuring misting sprays that fans can walk through to cool off. The heat and humidity here can be oppressive, and a stroll through the cool mist is great between the action—or, for the many children, *during* the action.

For the grown-ups, there is the Braves Chop House on the lower level in right center—a bar-restaurant with a meet-and-mingle atmosphere, for those more interested in socializing than in Bobby Cox's pitching changes.

Although the Braves have been among the leaders in attendance since the opening of the Ted, the team does not enjoy consistent sellouts. This could be a case of too much success: A sure bet for the playoffs every year since 1991, fans could be desensitized to the positive energy and congenial atmosphere found at Turner Field.

193

The first time I saw a major-league stadium from the inside was the first day I got called up to Atlanta last year.

So it was pretty awesome.

— KEVIN MILLWOOD

MELVIN MORA "Every field in the big leagues is a good field. I like Turner because of the lights; I can see the ball well. The grass in the outfield, the people, that's the first place I saw when I came to the big leagues."

TURK WENDELL "When I was a Cub, I was there for Opening Day ceremonies. One of the coolest things I've ever seen on the field was when they had an American bald eagle come down from the rafters in the upper deck down to home plate. It swooped around the field a couple of times—it was really exciting."

- ♦ *Home of the Atlanta Braves*
- ♦ *Atlanta, Georgia: Georgia Avenue, Pollard Boulevard, Bill Lucas Drive, and Hank Aaron Drive*
- ♦ *Built 1997*
- ♦ *Opening Day: March 29, 1997*
- ♦ *Cost: $235 Million*
- ♦ *Seating Capacity: 49,831 (1997); 49,714 (2000)*
- ♦ *Largest Crowd: 51,713 (October 1, 1998)*
- ♦ *Nickname: The Ted*

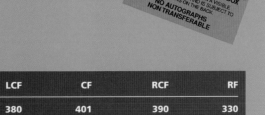

MARK GARDNER "A great improvement on Fulton County. It became more of a pitcher's park to right field. Left field, the ball still gets out of there pretty good. I think their hitters were a little disappointed in the field as far as the fences go. Balls weren't going out as much. Personally, I think it's a great field. It's one of my top five."

DIMENSIONS	LF	LCF	CF	RCF	RF
(1999)	325	380	401	390	330

Veterans Stadium

IT IS QUITE A SHOCK seeing an artificial-turf stadium in person for the first time—the shade of green that doesn't exist in nature; the absence of infield dirt, save for cutouts around the bases; the way ground balls up the middle can roll all the way to the wall and become triples. The Turf changes the game visually and viscerally. Fortunately, the fans in Philadelphia are scheduled to receive a new stadium with a natural grass surface.

To enter the Vet, you descend one or two levels, depending on seat location, after passing through the gate from the street. The playing field is sunken, which means the ballpark really holds the heat in warm weather. The Vet is a fully enclosed multipurpose stadium with many thousands of seats in the upper deck in fair territory. A given stadium's watchability quotient is sometimes expressed in the percentage of desirable foul-territory seats to not-so-desirable fair-territory seats. The Vet does not rank highly. While this stadium is impressive for its sheer capacity—sometimes in excess of 62,000—the view from the outfield upper deck is distant at best.

I was interviewing

Hall of Famer Mike Schmidt,

and the Phillies set my

shoelaces on fire.

It really made me feel like

one of the boys.

—**DAN GUTMAN (WRITER)**

◆ *Home of the Philadelphia Phillies*

◆ *Philadelphia, Pennsylvania: Broad Street, Pattison Avenue, Packer Street, and Tenth Street*

◆ *Built 1971*

◆ *Opening Day: April 10, 1971*

◆ *Cost: $50 Million*

◆ *Seating Capacity: 56,371 (1971); 62,382 (1990); 62,363 (2000)*

◆ *Largest Crowd: 67,064 (World Series, Game 5, October 16, 1983)*

◆ *Nickname: The Vet*

◆ *Home of NFL's Philadelphia Eagles*

DIMENSIONS	LF	LCF	CF	RCF	RF
(1991)	330	371	408	371	330

JOHN MABRY "I grew up around the Philadelphia area, so I went to Veterans Stadium as a little kid, so that was probably the first one I saw in person . . . You go out and you say, 'Wow.' You didn't think a baseball field could look this good or be this big. And you just look at it and stand there and take it all in for a minute, and it's just amazing to see."

VINNY CASTILLA "I was impressed the first time I was in a major-league field because it was my first day in the big leagues . . . I was with the Braves in '91, and the Braves were in the pennant race . . . Every game in September '91 when I got called up was a big game for the Braves . . . The stadium was packed, and you see the intensity on the bench. It was great because I never felt that in the minor leagues, and I felt that in my first game in the big leagues and I didn't even play—I was on the bench and I felt everything. Veterans Stadium, Philadelphia: That was my first stadium that I played in the big leagues."

RICH DELUCIA "My first time, I remember seeing Pete Rose run on the field during batting practice at Veterans Stadium in Philadelphia and seeing Steve Carlton and Mike Schmidt, those type of players in a big-league stadium. You walk down a dark tunnel and then you come out and it's all light, that's a really neat feeling, and I guess that's the way in any stadium, really, it's kind of dark inside, and then boom, you go in and it's like a big cathedral outside."

RICH AURILIA "Probably the most notorious fans are the fans at Veterans Stadium. They get on you pretty good. Luckily enough, I grew up in that kind of scenario, so I don't let it affect me. But you hear the guys around the clubhouse talk about some of the worst ragging coming from the fans. I think the New York fans are pretty harsh, but a lot of these guys say the Phillies [fans are worse]. I get a kick listening to some of the comments they make."

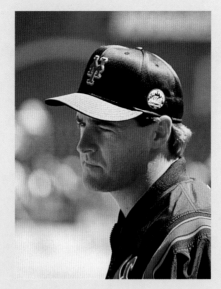

AL LEITER "I think the most vivid memory that I have is as a kid, going up the concourse at Veterans Stadium and seeing that green, *green* AstroTurf . . . Growing up at the Jersey shore, we used to make a lot of trips to the Vet, and I was impressed with the rug. I hate the rug now."

TODD KALAS (BROADCASTER) "Once we moved to Philadelphia in 1971 at age six, and all the way up through high school, Veterans Stadium kind of became my second home. It was where we spent our entire summers. You know, some kids go away to summer camps, some kids spend time with their grandparents. Basically, Veterans Stadium was where my brother and I grew up for about eleven summers. And it was tremendous. We would play in the bowels of the stadium, we would hit baseballs, we would play basketball; that was our playground. And it really didn't dawn on me until a few years into that whole process—as I got older, maybe into junior high school—just how special it was, to be able to call a ballpark your own. And to go in there every day and be around major-league players . . . Veterans Stadium still has a special place in my heart; I can tell you about all the nooks and crannies underneath that stadium because I've probably been there and gotten dirty and ruined pants and ruined shorts and had just a great time down there."

BOB WALK "My favorite memory as a player was: I got to the ballpark right in the middle of a game between the Phillies and the Astros. When I walked down the tunnel into the dugout with my uniform on for the first time, the very first thing I saw was back-to-back home runs by Schmidt and Luzinski. And that was my first experience sitting in a major-league dugout, so that was pretty exciting for me. I was like, 'Wow, this is an incredible ball team.' It was almost like an All-Star team, playing with those guys: Rose and Bowa, Trillo and Boone and Maddox, McBride—it was just a bunch of great players, I was really in awe of the whole thing. That was at the Vet, around Memorial Day. I think there was about fifty to sixty thousand people in there, little bit of a dynasty going there with the club."

Wrigley
Field

FOR ITS COMBINATION of beauty, intimacy, and ambience, one ballpark stands out in a league of its own: Wrigley. The experience is not limited to inside the stadium. The neighborhood around Wrigley, near Chicago's North Side, is appropriately called Wrigleyville, an indication of how baseball permeates the area. On game day, an electricity extends for many blocks in every direction, a sense of community that's found nowhere else in America's baseball cities. In the early twentieth century, baseball teams built their parks in the heart of their fan base. But one by one these inner-city neighborhoods deteriorated, and the clubs fled along with their fans to the suburbs. Not so in Wrigleyville, where pubs, bookstores, and clothing boutiques make this burg within a big city the funkiest, most livable ballpark neighborhood in any major-league city.

Wrigley Field is also the smallest and arguably the most intimate ballpark in the big leagues. Some parks may seem cozy from the front rows, but deep outfield fences, large foul territories, or steeply pitched upper decks can cause distant viewing in supposedly friendly confines—a phrase that is perfectly applied here. Built in 1914 and renovated several times, Wrigley has retained virtually all of its charm: ivy-covered walls, hand-operated scoreboard, sunswept bleachers. Even the Cubs' announcer Harry Caray was an icon. With his shock of white hair, oversize black-rimmed glasses, and gruff, folksy delivery, Caray was held in higher esteem than any of the Cubs players. A long-standing highlight of games here was Caray leading the crowd in a sing-along of "Take Me Out to the Ball Game" during the seventh-inning stretch. Corny, maybe, but fun nonetheless. Harry Caray passed away in 1998.

Wrigley is unmatched for its physical beauty. An afternoon game here must

203

JOE MANTEGNA (ACTOR) "To me, if somebody told you to invent the quintessential baseball stadium, it would be Wrigley Field. It's everybody's dream of what a baseball stadium should be. Unfortunately, the team doesn't quite come up to the standards of the park. . . . Can't have it all."

TODD HUNDLEY "You know, it's an overwhelming thing. Me growing up as a kid, it was Wrigley Field. Being in the city, and all of a sudden walking up the big corridor or stairs, it's all concrete, and then, boom! There's the green grass and the dirt . . . My dad [Randy Hundley] was done playing by the time I was old enough. I was born in '69, he was done in '74, '75. So me and my buddies would kind of miss school some days and get on a train and go down to the city."

RAFAEL PALMEIRO "I never did go to a big-league stadium as a child. The first big-league baseball stadium that I went to was when I was called up in Chicago when I was with the Cubs. I was overwhelmed when I came out on the field. I'd seen it many times on TV 'cause I followed the Cubs on WGN. And you see this great stadium on TV, then when you see it live, it's an amazing thing."

BRET SABERHAGEN "I was born in Chicago and lived out there for the first five years of my life. And my grandfather, who got me interested in baseball, was a Cubs fan. So my first big-league game was a doubleheader at Wrigley Field . . . Seeing Ernie Banks, Billy Williams, and Ron Santo and Don Kessinger, all the old Cubbies— that's what really got me liking the game—going out and watching it and seeing a beautiful ballpark."

◆ *Home of the Chicago Cubs*

◆ *Chicago, Illinois: North Clark Street, Waveland Avenue, Sheffield Avenue, and West Addison Street*

◆ *Built 1914*

◆ *Opening Day: April 23, 1914*

◆ *Cost: $250,000*

◆ *Seating Capacity: 38,710; 38,884 (2000)*

◆ *Largest Crowd: 46,965 (May 31, 1948)*

◆ *Nickname: The Friendly Confines*

◆ *Last major-league stadium to install lights, 1988*

DIMENSIONS	LF	LCF	CF	RCF	RF
(1914)	345	N/A	440	N/A	356
(1920)	348	N/A	447	N/A	318
(1991)	355	357	400	363	353

be why baseball was invented. The Cubbies have rarely fielded a contender in the past fifty years, but their fans remain loyal, consistently filling the stands. Part of the charm might be the consistency of their failure. You suspect they will lose in the end, yet hope still springs eternal on the near North Side.

After the first big-league night game was played in Cincinnati in 1935, teams gradually found that they could attract a bigger gate by playing games after most people finished work. In the mid-eighties, when the Cubs were making late-season noise, there was talk of moving their home World Series games across town to Comiskey Park or even to Milwaukee's County Stadium, since Wrigley did not have lights. The television networks had long ago decreed that all World Series games were to be played at night. So after much protesting, lights were installed in 1988. But the Cubs still have not played in the World Series since 1945.

My favorite is Wrigley Field. I played

my first major-league game in Wrigley,

got my first major-league hit, and I still

enjoy going there.

—MIKE PIAZZA

EDGARDO ALFONZO "I don't like it, I don't know why. Probably because of too many day games. For me, I don't see the ball pretty good over there. But the field's nice, don't get me wrong. But I don't feel comfortable there."

JERRY COLANGELO (DIAMONDBACKS OWNER) "Well, I must admit, [I was] seven or eight years old and happened to be at Wrigley Field in Chicago . . . It looked surreal. To be able to see the players after listening to them on radio—because that was before television. It was just a tremendous thrill."

TIM RAINES "The first stadium I ever saw was Wrigley Field, and that was three years out of high school, and I had never really been to a major-league stadium before. It was after my third year in the minors; the only stadiums I saw were minor-league stadiums . . . I was so in awe, and nervous—I couldn't hit a ball out of the cage, and I couldn't catch a fly ball in the outfield, I was that nervous."

BOB FRIEND "My very first memory of seeing a big-league park was very exciting. I was around seven or eight years old when my dad and I took a train from Lafayette, Indiana, to Chicago to see the Cubs in a doubleheader at Wrigley Field. The Cubs beat the Dodgers in the first game. The second game was called because of darkness. Some of the players on the field were Bill Lee, Gabby Hartnett, Phil Cavarretta, and Dolf Camilli.

"That beautiful ivy-covered fence and ballpark stands as one of my favorites today. I also had great success there—two one-hitters and a near perfect game in 1955, facing only twenty-seven men."

MIKE STANTON "My second big-league appearance, I was with Atlanta, we went into Wrigley. It was a pretty special moment for me, because I'd been watching the Cubs forever on WGN. Just stand out there and see the ivy . . . and see all the parts of the stadium that you didn't get to see from TV, it just made an impression on me, that this is where I want to be."

JIM HICKMAN "Wrigley Field was the best. You could smell the hot dogs and popcorn . . . The ivy, the grass, small dugouts, bleachers—everything was great."

CHIP CARAY (BROADCASTER) "One of my fondest memories is our family's claim to baseball history: three generations of major-league broadcasters together at the same time, May 13, 1996. My dad Skip and I were working for the Braves, my grandfather Harry for the Cubs . . . my first ever visit to Wrigley Field . . . The highlight . . . came in the seventh inning, when Harry sang 'Take Me Out to the Ball Game.' Seeing the joy, the love, the passion he and Cubs fans had for each other was just wonderful. I gave him a standing ovation with tears running down my face. And then a big hug to my dad—for the first time in a long time, I felt really connected . . . Now that my grandfather is gone, believe me, that day at Wrigley remains a cherished memory."

JIM THOME "It's the cream of the crop."

GENE ELSTON (BROADCASTER) "In 1934 my father purchased a new Chevrolet and announced we would break it in with a motor trip to Chicago to see the Cubs and St. Louis. Having heard many stories concerning the gangsters in the Windy City, I was quite uneasy upon our arrival—in the dead of night—while driving to our relatives' home. That was all forgotten the next morning when I found myself in a lower box seat at Wrigley Field on the first-base line behind the Cardinals' dugout, and Dizzy Dean would be the St. Louis pitcher. This thrill turned into another, twenty years later, 1954 on Labor Day. I would be sitting in the Cubs broadcast booth with Bert Wilson and broadcasting my first big-league game—the first of forty-two seasons of calling Major League Baseball."

GENE LAMONT "The first [big-league stadium] I saw as a child was Wrigley Field. It seemed awfully big, just the field and everything, how nice the field was manicured and everything. We had, in Illinois, skin infields, no grass on the infields. I was really impressed."

JOE CARTER "The first stadium that really impressed me the most was the first one I played in—that was Wrigley Field. To have all the history and

to go there and have the ivy climbing the walls . . . You couldn't believe that you were finally on a ballpark field that you had seen on TV so much."

Yankee
Stadium

THE NEW YORK YANKEES didn't always play in the most famous stadium in the world. In fact, they weren't always called the Yankees. In 1903, a team called the Baltimore Orioles moved to New York and changed their name to the Highlanders, after their new home field, Hilltop Park, situated on elevated land at West 165th Street at the northern end of Manhattan, now the site of Columbia-Presbyterian Hospital. Legend has it that a few years later the New York sportswriters grew tired of trying to squeeze this lengthy name into headlines and began calling the team the Yankees.

Hilltop was a small, deteriorating field. So the Yankees happily accepted the 1913 offer by the New York Giants of the National League to share their home park, Polo Grounds, only a short distance away at West 155th Street. The Yankees were welcome there until 1921 when, with the help of an exciting young slugger named Babe Ruth, the team outdrew their hosts by 350,000 fans. This prompted Giants owner Charles Stoneham to evict the Yankees, effective at the end of the 1922 season. The owners of the Yankees then purchased a ten-acre parcel of land in the Bronx, across the Harlem River and just south of Polo Grounds. It was there that they erected the House That Ruth Built—at that time the grandest ballpark ever built. And it remains so.

Prior to Yankee Stadium, baseball parks were mostly pastoral sites, with small wooden grandstands. Though these fields were built in the midst of cities, the game wasn't as popular as it would become, and large stadiums weren't needed. The Babe, with his ability to hit prodigious home runs and his larger-than-life image, changed all that. As he became one of the great American heroes, Ruth brought attention to the sport. Fans responded, turning a mostly rural game into America's pastime and ushering in the era of large stadiums.

211

BOB COSTAS (BROADCASTER) "First time I remember: September 1959, Baltimore at New York. I'm seven. My dad takes me to Yankee Stadium. Orioles beat Yanks, 7–2. Mantle doesn't play. After watching baseball on black-and-white TV, the field, base paths, stands—everything looks so vivid that it's almost breathtaking for a little kid. After the game, they let you leave by way of the warning track. We got to the monuments in center field and I was pretty sure they were tombstones—the burial places of Huggins, Ruth, and Gehrig. Would Mantle and Joe D. someday rest there, too? It was a bit much for a kid to contemplate."

DEREK JETER "Yankee Stadium—it was gigantic. Everything looked so, *so* big. I mean, that's pretty much what I remember. It seemed larger than life."

RAY ROBINSON (AUTHOR) "I was taken to my first major-league game at Yankee Stadium by my next-door neighbor, who I'm sure was a Prohibition-era bootlegger. I was about eight years old at the time, and my elderly companion kept telling me to keep my eyes on Babe Ruth. Instead, I kept watching Lou Gehrig, who had played at Columbia, which was across the street from my apartment house. Sure enough, Lou hit a line-drive homer that day. The other fellow I couldn't take my eyes off was Herb Pennock, for whom the term 'stylish southpaw' had to be invented. I haven't the slightest notion who won that day—the Yankees were playing the great Philadelphia Athletics—but the enormity of the stadium, the constant roar and growling of the large crowd, and the smoke that descended over the field late in the afternoon is something I'll never forget."

TINO MARTINEZ "Yankee Stadium, in the 1981 World Series. My dad brought me and my brother to the game here, and it's the first time I really walked into a major-league stadium. I was fourteen years old."

When I first saw Yankee Stadium I thought, "Boy, this place is big!"

— YOGI BERRA

Since the Babe, the Yankees have stood for a winning tradition. From 1921 to 1964, the Yankees played in twenty-nine World Series. More seasons than not, the Yanks were vying for the Championship. They expected to win, and so did their fans.

The dynasty ended in 1965, a result of poor management. With the advent of the amateur draft, the Yanks could no longer merely sign any young, talented player at will, and the organization lacked quality replacements for their aging roster. In 1973, George Steinbrenner bought the team and endeavored to restore the Yankees' luster. They've since won six World Championships—not a bad record in the free-agency era. All this success, however, has not always translated to ticket sales, which have been hampered by the lack of parking, highway traffic jams, and the allegedly unsafe neighborhood. Once inside, though, there is nothing else like it in baseball—or in all of sports, for that matter.

JASON DICKSON "First big-league stadium . . . was when I first got called up to the big leagues: Yankee Stadium. I was a Yankees fan my whole life growing up, so I was in Yankee Stadium pitching against the Yankees . . . It was pretty amazing."

ROLLIE SHELDON "This sure beats Auburn, New York, and Woodstock Academy, Connecticut. After I signed, the Yankees invited me to the stadium to work with Ed Lopat before going to Class D ball. As I sat in the stands watching a game later, Moose Skowron hit a low liner to right field that got to the 407-foot auxiliary scoreboard so quick it seemed unreal. I had a feeling I was overmatched, and these players were in a league of their own. Luckily, I made the jump from Class D to the stadium the very next year, 1961."

MARK MCGWIRE "My first real game in the big leagues was Yankee Stadium. So I was pretty proud of that. But you can't psychologically go, 'Oh, my God, this is historically one of the greatest stadiums in the world . . . I understand that 'Hey, this is just a stadium.' I can't get caught up in the history; I've got to play the game of baseball."

♦ *Home of the New York Yankees*

♦ *Bronx, New York: East 157th Street, River Avenue, East 161st Street, and Ruppert Place*

♦ *Built 1923*

♦ *Opening Day: April 18, 1923*

♦ *Cost: $2.5 Million*

♦ *Closed for renovation September 30, 1973; reopened April 15, 1976; estimated renovation cost $100–$200 million*

♦ *Seating Capacity: 58,000 (1923); 67,337 (1961); 57,545 (1993)*

♦ *Largest Crowd, Old Stadium: 85,265 (September 9, 1928)*

♦ *Largest Crowd, New Stadium: 57,545 (October 14, 1999)*

♦ *Nickname: The House That Ruth Built*

♦ *Former home of NFL's New York Giants*

BUCK SHOWALTER "First time I was in Yankee Stadium . . . it was breathtaking. I think baseball separates itself from all other sports, where I think it's one of the few sports where fans go to a game to see the venue, to see the stadium, as opposed to, sometimes, to see the game . . . It's a place where you can have a conversation with your son or daughter, and you can spend the time well."

DIMENSIONS	LF	LCF	CF	RCF	RF
(1923)	301	457	461	367	296
(1990)	318	399	408	385	314

JIM LEYLAND "Yankee Stadium, first major-league game, coach for White Sox: scared to death."

STANLEY COHEN (AUTHOR) "Having grown up in the Bronx, just a few subway stops from Yankee Stadium, I had seen the ballpark many times, but never from the inside. I had caught glimpses of the field from the elevated as it passed 161st Street on its way into or out of the intestines of New York's subway system. But that was small preparation for what confronted me on my first visit. The expanse of green that stretched before me seemed endless. It was more grass than I had ever seen before, interrupted only by the smooth rust-colored dirt of the infield and the pitcher's mound and a grassless channel that led from the mound to home plate. This was the original Yankee Stadium, the field framed by three tiers of grandstands that rose to a forbidding height, capped by a sweeping roof from which hung a frieze of white battlements and which cast deep shadows across the seats beneath it. It was an altogether ominous sight for a nine-year-old, and as I looked into the recesses of the upper deck, I was grateful to be sitting at ground level, under the gray light of a cloud-ridden sky. It was the first of hundreds of visits, several years before light stanchions were added to the roof, three decades before the stadium was remodeled. There has never been, and probably never will be, another ballpark like it. If the great ballplayers of the ages—Ruth and Cobb, DiMaggio and Williams, Mays and Mantle—were ever to be resurrected to play one game for all eternity, that game would be played in the old Yankee Stadium."

GEORGE MITTERWALD "Watching Yankee Stadium on TV gives no real perspective of how awe-inspiring it is when you actually see it in person for the first time, like I did in 1966 as a twenty-one-year-old. This was before they modernized it. The first thing you want to do is go to the monuments in center field, on the playing field, and see Frank Howard's double that rattled around behind them at 461 feet."

STEVE BLASS "My first experience with a major-league ballpark was at Yankee Stadium. I grew up in a town of about five hundred people in upstate Connecticut. So I was thrilled to take the train down, and I'd never been around a big ballpark before in my life. And I came through one of the tunnels, I saw the big lights and I saw the emerald-green grass, and I thought I'd gone to heaven. I'd never seen anything so pretty in my life. And I've never seen anything so pretty since."

JOHNNY BLANCHARD "The first time I saw Yankee Stadium, it was full. Needless to say, I was scared to death. Fifty-eight thousand people . . . My thought was, what was I doing here?"

STAN KASTEN (EXECUTIVE) "I was nine and living in New Jersey, and whenever I'd visit relatives in the Bronx, we'd go past Yankee Stadium. And there was just a sliver of the field you could see when you were on the train, just between the right-field stands and where the signage began. So you'd always see the grass, a little hint of grass before you got to the field, and for years, since I was tiny, I wanted to see it. Then it was during the 1961 season, my uncle finally took me. We got into bleacher seats, and I remember looking through the portal and the very first thing I saw was the number 1 on Bobby Richardson's back. From coming through the center-field bleachers—that was the angle—and I see the number 1 and I know it's Bobby Richardson, and I remember that like it was yesterday."

RICK CERONE "I remember my dad, we drove over from Newark, New Jersey, to Yankee Stadium. I was in Little League at the time, and you're used to Little League fields. Then all of a sudden, you walk through the entrance and I remember walking up the little corridor or hallway, then seeing this big, big ballpark. And the green grass is what I'll always remember, how green it was, and it was greener than anything I ever played on. And then it was overwhelming because it was so big and it was just a beautiful sight. We enjoyed our first game, we actually sat behind the press box and I got a foul ball by Norm Siebern. He . . . was fouling balls off all day. Left-hander, Kansas City Athletics. Fouling 'em back, fouling 'em back, just all around our area. And I kept missing them, I couldn't get one. Last one he fouls off, around the eighth inning, goes right into the broadcast booth. Phil Rizzuto catches it, turns around, and hands it to me. In my first game! Years later I got to work with Scooter, he was my partner with WPIX. And also, my first year with the Yankees in '80, I got Norm Siebern to sign a baseball. So I've kept the Norm Siebern ball. It wasn't the same ball . . . but the circle was definitely complete."

TOM VERDUCCI (WRITER) "My first memory of Yankee Stadium was going to see the Washington Senators play the Yankees. I believe that Dick Nen hit a ball behind the monuments in center field. It was an inside-the-park home run. I thought it was something that happened all the time. Now that I look back, I realize how special it was."

The Yankee Stadium of today is not the same ballpark as it was before the renovation of 1974–1975, a thorough reconstruction that removed much of its unique look. The monuments to Babe Ruth, Lou Gehrig, and Miller Huggins that stood in play in center field were placed behind the left-center-field wall in a lovely enclosed space called Monument Park. The concrete roof that overhung and encircled the stadium was removed, as were the two auxiliary scoreboards located at the base of the outfield walls. Still, the place enthralls. When you emerge from the tunnel, you cannot help but be awed by the majestic expanse, echoing greatness from decades past. No matter how often you walk through those gates, no matter where you sit, the feeling is there, thrilling yet humbling.

PETE VAN WIEREN (BROADCASTER) "The
first Major League Baseball stadium I saw was the old
Yankee Stadium when I was a kid. I think I was about
eleven or twelve years old, and most of the baseball I
was familiar with was baseball games I'd heard on the
radio, or I occasionally saw a World Series game or a
Game of the Week on television. So when you walk
into that major-league ballpark for the first time, and
it's that particular ballpark, with all those great Yankees teams back in the fifties, it was like heaven to
me, that was the greatest thing I had ever seen. I
grew up in Rochester, New York. It was during a
family vacation in New York City. We went to a
Yankee-Tigers doubleheader. I even know Whitey
Ford pitched the first game of that doubleheader. I'll
never forget that."

REX HUDLER "When I got to the big leagues,
playing in Yankee Stadium, being a Yankee, growing
up there and walking through the tunnels to get to
the clubhouse, it was dark in the clubhouse, I could
feel the spirits of Babe Ruth, Mickey Mantle, all the
great players. As I walked to the clubhouse, opened
up the door to Yankee Stadium and all the white pin-
striped jerseys were hanging, it was like a ray of light
come beaming out of that locker room."

Photo Credits

All photographs © by Ira Rosen except the following: